Some
Do 'Ave 'Em

by Guy Unsworth

Based on the TV series by
Raymond Allen

‖SAMUEL FRENCH‖

FOR AMATEUR PRODUCTION ENQUIRIES

UNITED KINGDOM AND WORLD
EXCLUDING NORTH AMERICA
licensing@concordtheatricals.co.uk

020-7054-7298

Each title is subject to availability from Concord Theatricals, depending upon country of performance.

This work is published by Samuel French, an imprint of Concord Theatricals. Ltd

The Professional Rights in this play are controlled by Alan Brodie Representation, Paddock Suite, The Courtyard, 55 Charterhouse Street, London, EC1M 6HA, alan@alanbrodie.com / abr@alanbrodie.com. Tel: +44 (0) 20 7253 6226..

USE OF COPYRIGHTED MUSIC

USE OF COPYRIGHTED THIRD-PARTY MATERIALS

IMPORTANT BILLING AND CREDIT REQUIREMENTS

SOME MOTHERS DO 'AVE 'EM was first performed at the Wyvern Theatre, Swindon on 21 February 2018 ahead of a UK Tour. It was produced by Limelight Productions. The cast was as follows:

FRANK SPENCER	Joe Pasquale
BETTY SPENCER	Sarah Earnshaw
FATHER O'HARA	David Shaw-Park
BARBARA FISHER	Susie Blake
DAVID WORTHINGTON / TERRY LUSCOMBE	Moray Treadwell
CAMERA OPERATOR / CONSTABLE / US FRANK SPENCER	Chris Kiely

UNDERSTUDIES

BETTY SPENCER / BARBARA FISHER	Leoni Kibbey
MR LUSCOMBE / MR WORTHING / FATHER O'HARA / CAMERA OPERATOR / CONSTABLE	Peter F Gardiner

CREATIVE TEAM

Written and Directed by	**GUY UNSWORTH**
Based on the original TV series by	**RAYMOND ALLEN**
Set & Costume Design	**SIMON HIGLETT**
Lighting Design	**MATT HASKINS**
Sound Design	**IAN HORROCKS-TAYLOR**
Casting	**EMILY JONES**
Choreography	**JENNY ARNOLD**
Stunt Co-ordinator	**KEV MCCURDY**

PRODUCTION TEAM

General Management	**LIMELIGHT PRODUCTIONS**
Production Manager	**JILL ASHALL**
Costume Supervisor	**MISCHABEL WAKEMAN-READ**
Company Stage Manager	**NIK RYAL**
Deputy Stage Manager	**AMY CLARKE**
Assistant Stage Manager	**DAVID WILLIAMS**
Sound Operator	**SIMON HAWKINS**
Chief LX (Touring)	**TERESA NAGEL**
Wardrobe Mistress	**HILDA GREENWOOD**
Production Carpenter	**DANIEL GAVIN-MILLS**

CHARACTERS

(In order of appearance)

FRANK SPENCER – (30–50)

BETTY SPENCER – Frank's Wife (25–40)

FATHER O'HARA – An Irish Catholic Priest (55–75)

BARBARA FISHER – Betty's Mother (50–65)

DAVID WORTHINGTON – A Scottish Bank Manager (50–65)

TERRY LUSCOMBE – BBC Entertainment Chief (50–65)

LESLIE ROBIN – A Camera operator (25–45)

CONSTABLE – A London Policeman (25–45)

The play is performed by six actors. The following roles are doubled: Mr Worthington/Mr Luscombe and Leslie/Constable.

The roles of Leslie and Constable can be played by any gender. Spelling and pronouns should be adjusted accordingly (I.e Lesley Robin)

SETTING

At the house of Frank and Betty Spencer.

TIME

The action takes place in real time one evening in the spring of 1974. Subheadings are included in the script for ease of rehearsals. The action, however, is continuous.

AUTHOR'S NOTE

Born in the late eighties, I wasn't one of the twenty-six million who watched Some Mothers Do 'Ave 'Em at its peak, but by accident caught re-runs of it as a teenager. Slapstick had always made me laugh and I remember finding Frank Spencer utterly hilarious.

Years later, I re-watched the episodes and fell in love with it once more. I was struck not only by the daring stunts, but by a great heart at the centre of it. Here were two characters, so brilliantly played by Michael Crawford and Michele Dotrice, who had no money, no house of their own, no job, no hope of a job, but they had each other. And whether Frank got the sack, demolished their home, or gave his psychiatrist a mental breakdown, there was always a very real and poignant relationship between these two individuals who totally adored each other. This struck a chord with me far beyond the enjoyment of a twenty-five-minute episode, and suggested that maybe, just maybe, we could spend an evening with Frank and Betty in a theatre.

A few years later at the Playhouse Theatre in the West End, I was the Associate Director on the Monty Python musical *Spamalot*. Joe Pasquale was playing King Arthur. On a sweltering afternoon in June 2013, Joe and I stood in front of an electric fan in the green room trying to cool down, but it was clear that the fan was completely useless. Joe bent down to fix it when, at the lightest of touches, the entire contraption fell to pieces. We both laughed and referenced Frank Spencer, and in that brief moment discovered our mutual love of Some Mothers.

To cut a very long story short, we managed to make contact with Raymond Allen, original writer of the TV series, and asked if we could visit him at home on the Isle of Wight where Joe happened to be performing in his stand-up tour. A message came back from Ray: "I love Joe Pasquale, I've already booked tickets for his show, I'll see you there". That was about it. I think that Ray, the kindest gentleman you could find, was so pleased with the idea of Joe playing Frank that, without further ado, I found myself creating a stage play of one of my favourite TV shows, with one of my favourite comedians and collaborators.

To Ray for trusting me, thank you. To Joe for being there every single step of the way, I'm eternally grateful.

That was autumn 2015, after which I set about writing a first draft. I wanted the play to be nostalgic – a homage to the time, style and music of the original, but specifically written for the stage rather than lifted directly from the TV series. The trickiest part was incorporating the stunts and, more to the point, sustaining the Some Mothers format for a full length play without it feeling like a dragged-out episode. I'd grown up watching great comedies on stage, from Ayckbourn to Cooney, Frayn to Feydeau, so I was keen to honour the style which had always worked so well in the theatre. But my first draft was wildly out of proportion: there were multiple locations, three actors on roller skates, lamp-posts, collapsing roofs, real (and loose) chickens, and far too many script dead-ends.

Through multiple redrafts, two rehearsed readings and a week of workshopping the show, the final draft of the play was tighter and funnier, and, in the hands of my superb set designer Simon Higlett, stageable. Incidentally, and useful to anyone putting the show on themselves, we discovered very early on that there was no mileage in doing impressions of the original actors. However skilful, no one could match the real Michael Crawford, and in any case the novelty of an impersonation would wear off very quickly.

In this case it would also have been a missed opportunity, as I was lucky to have the charming naivety which Joe Pasquale naturally brings in bucketloads. Also, Joe's relationship with the wonderfully warm Sarah Earnshaw as Betty (Sarah had already played opposite Joe in *Spamalot*) was evidently touching in its own, unique way. I was lucky to be able to reinvent Frank's mother-in-law for the brilliantly skilled Susie Blake, whilst Moray Treadwell, David Shaw-Parker and Chris Kiely heroically rose to the challenge as the straight men to Frank's mayhem. Impressions were out, but Frank and Betty's world still firmly remained.

My sincere thanks goes to the many brilliant and talented individuals who contributed to the development process with such skill and good humour, to Theatre Royal Bath for generously supporting the second reading and workshop, and to Limelight Productions for enthusiastically taking on the challenge of producing the show. A special thank you must go to Christopher Luscombe who so tirelessly contributed as a friend, mentor and script consultant throughout the whole process.

In February 2018 we began rehearsals for a UK tour and, with such a verbally and physically demanding piece, the cast all agreed to arrive on day one word-perfect. They did so, brilliantly, and it was the best decision we ever made. Three and a half weeks later, we opened the UK tour in Swindon. From the moment the curtain went up, there was a palpable sense that the audience was happy to be back in the charming, cosy, carefree world of Frank and Betty's living room. With different actors, yes, but with characters they knew well and were extremely fond of. The stunts were great highlights, the seventies music went down a treat, and the terrific cast exuded charm from start to finish.

However, as the final moments of the play drew to a close, I was reminded once again of the thing which had attracted me to *Some Mothers Do 'Ave 'Em* many years ago: that all the chaos aside, Ray Allen had provided us with one of the great British love stories. Frank and Betty showed us, and continue to show us, that even when the world around us is falling apart, a little bit of love will conquer anything.

To everyone who gave a little bit of love to this – and you know who you are – thank you.

Guy Unsworth

ACT I

(Spring, 1974.)

(The ground floor of **FRANK** *and* **BETTY**'s *house. We can see the living room and stairs.)*

(On the wall is a framed poster of Engelbert Humperdinck, an unframed poster of Bruce Forsyth, and a smaller framed picture of Jesus. On the floor is a homemade Wendy house.)

*(***FATHER O'HARA** *and* **BETTY** *are having a cup of tea.)*

TEA WITH FATHER O'HARA

FATHER O'HARA. I know Mr Spencer has a tendency to worry, but I think it's best to tell him sooner rather than later, don't you?

BETTY. He's been having a hard time recently. Looking for work, and no money coming in. I'm sorry, Father, I just get so worried.

FATHER O'HARA. Try not to be anxious, Mrs Spencer. It's just a case of taking things easy and getting plenty of rest. And Doctor Smedley can always prescribe a tonic.

BETTY. Oh yes! That would really help him.

FATHER O'HARA. Not for Frank, for you! You don't think it will come as a surprise to him do you?

BETTY. Oh yes it's bound to, I told him I was off to the dentist.

FATHER O'HARA. Mrs Spencer, your husband does *want* a child, doesn't he?

BETTY. Of course he does. It's just that we've been trying so hard. For so long. And he lost his job this week.

FATHER O'HARA. Oh dear. How did he cope with that?

BETTY. The same as last week.

FATHER O'HARA. I see. It must be hard for you both but I'm sure things will settle down.

BETTY. He's been trying for a job at the Civic Hall today.

FATHER O'HARA. Oh, are they looking for new cleaners?

BETTY. No, he's been auditioning.

FATHER O'HARA. Auditioning?

BETTY. For Mr Lockwood's magic show.

FATHER O'HARA. Mr Lockwood's – right – Frank's a... right.

BETTY. He'll be home any minute actually.

FATHER O'HARA. Then I must do a disappearing act too. I'm off to the Civic Hall *myself* tonight.

BETTY. Oh, is there a concert?

FATHER O'HARA. No no it's a gang show. I thought we should raise some money after the Civic was broken into last month.

BETTY. Oh yes, I heard, terrible.

FATHER O'HARA. *(Top secret.)* Six and a half thousand pounds they took!

BETTY. Goodness.

FATHER O'HARA. Anyway, thank you for the tea.

BETTY. Thank you for dropping in, Father – I hope it wasn't out of your way.

FATHER O'HARA. Not at all. *(Referring to the Wendy House.)* Is this a Wendy House? You're not receiving gifts already are you?

BETTY. Oh that's not for the baby, Father – Frank made it for the chickens.

FATHER O'HARA. The chickens?!

> *(The sound of a key in the front door.)*

BETTY. That must be Frank now.

FRANK ARRIVES HOME

> (**FRANK** *enters in trench coat and beret. He is holding his magic case.)*

FRANK. Hello Betty, I'm home.

BETTY. Hello, Frank. We've got a visitor.

FATHER O'HARA. Good evening, Mr Spencer.

FRANK. Oh hello, Father O'Hara, what a lovely surprise. Doing the rounds are you?

BETTY. Father O'Hara just popped in for a cup of tea, Frank.

FRANK. Oh nice. And does my eye deceive me, Father, or are you admiring my new development?

FATHER O'HARA. Well, yes it's very... impressive Mr Spencer, but you can't keep chickens in the living room.

FRANK. Chick*en*.

FATHER O'HARA. I'm sorry?

FRANK. *(Whispering.)* Sshh. Mr Lindbergh is now a widower.

FATHER O'HARA. *(Whispering.)* Mr Lindbergh? What is he talking about?

BETTY. *(Whispering.)* The chicken, Father. There was an unfortunate accident at the weekend involving *Mrs* Lindbergh.

FATHER O'HARA. *(Whispering.) Mrs* Lindbergh?

FRANK. *(Whispering.) Mrs* Lindbergh, God bless her, had a visit from a greedy fox on Sunday, and was, let's just say, taken before her time.

FATHER O'HARA. *(Whispering.)* Well I'm sorry to hear that, but –

> (**FRANK** *lifts up the chimney gently as* **FATHER O'HARA** *peers in.)*

FRANK. Mr Lindbergh, this is Father O'Hara. Father O'Hara, this is Mr Lindbergh.

> *(With a squawk, feathers burst out into* **FATHER O'HARA***'s face.)*

He's going through a rough patch, father, it's a difficult time.

FATHER O'HARA. But these are not his natural surroundings, Mr Spencer. You don't want social services to find out you're keeping a rooster in your living room – they'll send the police round.

FRANK. The police?! Oh, I better put him outside then. I hope Mr fox doesn't return for a second sitting.

FATHER O'HARA. *(To* **BETTY,** *heading towards the front door.)* Mrs Spencer, I really must go, I need to eat before I head out.

BETTY. Of course. Father O'Hara's off to the Civic Hall *himself* tonight, Frank.

FRANK. Oh, is there a concert?

FATHER O'HARA. No no it's a gang show. I thought we should raise some money after the Civic was broken into last month.

FRANK. Oh yes, I heard, terrible.

FATHER O'HARA. *(Top secret.)* Six and a half thousand pounds they took!

FRANK. Goodness.

BETTY. Frank used to help out at the gang show, didn't you Frank?

FRANK. Yes the last time I was at a gang show, the scout master swallowed his woggle and I had to perform the Heineken manoeuvre on him.

BETTY. Why don't you stay and have supper here, Father? You could then go straight to the Civic Hall.

FRANK. Yes we're already expecting Betty's mother, so the more the merrier.

FATHER O'HARA. Oh right, I see, well that'd be lovely!

FRANK. And I'm cooking!

FATHER O'HARA. – But I need to sort out a few things at home.

FRANK. Betty's not been feeling herself lately so I'm stepping in. *(To* **BETTY.***)* It's all them carrots you've been munching. *(To* **FATHER O'HARA.***)* All she ever eats – carrots!

BETTY. If you change your mind, Father, you're more than welcome.

FATHER O'HARA. Thank you, and do give your mother my regards.

(To **FRANK.***)*

Look after her now won't you, Mr Spencer?

FRANK. *(Offended.)* Excuse me?

FATHER O'HARA. She'll need looking after if she's not feeling so good, won't she?

FRANK. *(Pert.)* Yes, thank you, father. You are not a doctor are you not?

FATHER O'HARA. I'm sorry?

FRANK. You are not, are you not, not a doctor are you not?

FATHER O'HARA. What?

BETTY. *(Gently reprimanding.)* Frank.

FATHER O'HARA. I'm sorry I don't think I –

BETTY. Don't worry, Father. Goodbye.

FATHER O'HARA. Right, goodbye then.

FRANK. Yes, goodbye.

BETTY. *(Calling after him.)* Thank you!

> *(**FATHER O'HARA** leaves. **BETTY** closes the front door.)*

WHAT WAS ALL THAT ABOUT?

What was all that about?

FRANK. Funny man.

BETTY. Father O'Hara?

FRANK. Telling me to look after you like that.

BETTY. He's only trying to help, Frank.

FRANK. I'm always looking after you. He doesn't need to tell me to do it. I just do do it, don't I?

BETTY. I know you do, Frank, but he didn't mean it like that –

FRANK. I'm a man!

BETTY. Frank, he was actually referring to a bit of news I got today.

FRANK. Nothing serious I hope. Not after the day I've had.

BETTY. Oh sorry Frank, I forgot to ask – how did the audition go? You tell me *your* news and I'll tell you *mine.*

FRANK. *(Defeated.)* You know how nervous I get when I'm performing.

BETTY. All performers get nervous, Frank.

FRANK. But the other magicians are more impressive than me. They all wear top hats! And tails! They escape from metal cages, make birds appear out of nowhere, while I'm stood juggling in front of Mr Lockwood, knowing that my balls are misshapen and my wand is smaller than everyone else's.

BETTY. What about your new trick? How did that go? Did you make his watch disappear?

FRANK. Well you *could* say it went better than usual.

BETTY. I bet Mr Lockwood had no idea where it went.

FRANK. No he didn't.

BETTY. So what was the problem?

FRANK. Neither did I.

BETTY. But you found his watch in the end didn't you?

FRANK. Nearly.

BETTY. Nearly?

FRANK. Not really.

BETTY. Frank!

FRANK. But I said to him, "Mr Lockwood, it will appear when you least expect it". And then I left.

BETTY. You left? What did he say?

FRANK. He said, "Give me back my watch, you silly man, or I'll tell your mother!" Only he used different words for "Silly"... And "Man" ... And "I'll tell your mother".

BETTY. Oh Frank!

FRANK. His face went bright red and his breathing was very erotic.

BETTY. I'm not surprised.

FRANK. So that's *another* job I won't be getting.

(**BETTY** *starts to clear the tea from earlier.*)

BETTY. Don't be like that Frank, you've only been out of work two days. Mr Rogers next door hasn't worked for six months.

FRANK. Mr Rogers is eighty three years old!

BETTY. Yes but he likes to keep active doesn't he? And he's still got all his faculties.

FRANK. *I've* got all *my* faculties. Young ones all raring to go. But nowhere to facultate.

BETTY. Oh Frank.

(*She takes the tea into the kitchen.* **FRANK** *slightly adjusts the picture of Jesus to straighten it. As he turns to walk away he places his hand on the banister knob, which comes out. He replaces it and the lamp by the door flickers.* **FRANK** *smacks the wall the other side of the door and it stops.* **FRANK** *looks inside his trousers, concerned.* **BETTY** *comes out.*)

It won't get any smaller just by looking at it.

FRANK. It's gone all the way round the back now.

BETTY. Let me have a look.

(*Looking into his trousers.*)

I can barely see it. I don't know what you're worrying about.

FRANK. *(Scratching.)* It keeps moving that's why.

BETTY. Well stop touching it, or it's bound to get bigger.

FRANK. My mother said if both ends join up you drop down dead.

BETTY. That's an old wive's tale. A rash won't kill you. And it's the worry that's brought it on.

FRANK. What do you expect, Betty? We need money. But I won't *find* that money if I don't get any work as a magician and I won't get any work as a magician if I don't find some money to improve my act. *(On the side nearby.)* And look at these heating bills. They're rising excrementally!

BETTY. Are you saying that's *my* fault?

FRANK. No-no-no. But we've got to economise. The whole country's facing a slump. And we're slumping quicker than the country.

> (**BETTY** *heads upstairs and* **FRANK** *runs after her.)*

BETTY. It's just as bad for me. I don't enjoy seeing you worried. I'm doing the best I can to save money.

FRANK. No-no-no I didn't mean that Betty.

BETTY. You're always criticising me.

FRANK. Please Betty!

BETTY. I don't want to discuss this any more –

FRANK. *(Sternly stopping her.)* Betty! Don't make me run! It gives me the cramps.

THAT'LL BE THE PHONE

> *(The phone rings.)*

That'll be the phone.

BETTY. It's probably Mum.

FRANK. You get the phone, I'll start dinner.

   (**FRANK** *goes into the kitchen.*)

BETTY. *(Picking up the phone.)* Grays-Thurrock-Five-double-six-seven-o? ... Hello Mum... Yes he's home now he's just started cooking.

   (Bang/crash from the kitchen.)

   (Whispering.)

Have I told him? I've not had the chance yet... Yes I know, I know... Mr Worthington? Well yes of course... All right we'll see you around half past seven...yes see you shortly. Bye. *(Calling.)* That was Mum, Frank. She's bringing Mr Worthington with her.

FRANK. *(From the kitchen.)* Mr Worthington?

   (Opening the hatch.)

"Mr-Worthington-from-the-bank" Mr Worthington? Mr Worthington of "Worthington-and-Sons" Mr Worthington?! Why's he coming here?

BETTY. Mum's met him a few times now and, well I think... You know...

FRANK. To what are you alluring?

BETTY. Well, they've become... "Good friends" to one another.

FRANK. *(Offended.)* "Good friends" eh? No wink nor nudge required, Betty Fisher. When I think what married people get up to these days!

BETTY. Mr Worthington lost his wife a few years back, and Dad's not exactly around anymore is he? Listen it's none of our business so don't make a thing of it. Besides, Mr Worthington's been very helpful to Mum.

FRANK. *(A bright idea.)* And he could be very helpful to us, Betty. If I can get Mr Worthington to invest in my costume and equitment for Magic Frank, we'll have the answer to all our life problems. With Magic Frank flying high, we'd have money in the meter, real flowers in the vase, Brucie in a frame. And as he's coming to see us here, I can integrate my magic record player too. Stamp your foot, Betty!

BETTY. Frank.

FRANK. Go on, Betty, stamp your foot!

BETTY. Not now, Frank.

FRANK. All right, *I* will.

> *(He stamps his foot and mysterious music plays: A song in the style of* ["**ALBATROSS**"] *by Fleetwood Mac.*)*

> *(Mysterious voice.)*

Ladies and Gentlemen, welcome to the world of Magic Frank.

BETTY. Very good Frank, but could we have a chat before they arrive?

FRANK. For my first trick, I will make your watch disappear in front of your very eye.

BETTY. Frank, they'll be here soon.

---

* A licence to produce SOME MOTHERS DO 'AVE 'EM does not include a performance licence for "ALBATROSS". The publisher and author suggest that the licensee contact PRS to ascertain the music publisher and contact such music publisher to license or acquire permission for performance of the song. If a licence or permission is unattainable for "ALBATROSS", the licensee may not use the song in SOME MOTHERS DO 'AVE 'EM but should create an original composition in a similar style or use a similar song in the public domain. For further information, please see Music Use Note on page iii.

FRANK.   Perhaps you would like to volunteer, Mr Worthington?

> (**BETTY** *stamps to stop the record player, but it skips to song in the style of* ["**CHIRPY CHIRPY CHEEP CHEEP**"] *by Middle of the Road.**)

Ooh it's my favourite!

> (**BETTY** *stamps to stop it again, and it skips once more to a song in the style of* ["**DUELING BANJOS**"] *by Eric Weissberg and Steve Mandell.*)

Ah it's cowboy time!

> (**BETTY** *rushes to the player and stops it.*)

> (*John Wayne.*)

Get off your horse and drink your milk.

> (**BETTY** *is clearly upset.*)

Now don't cry, Betty. Betty, what are you crying for?

BETTY. I can't help it Frank.

FRANK. (*Bolstering her.*) Here, do you remember what I used to do, when you got upset when we were courting? Do you remember? Yes you do, I can see it in your eyes.

---

* A licence to produce SOME MOTHERS DO 'AVE 'EM does not include a performance licence for "CHIRPY CHIRPY CHEEP CHEEP" and "DUELING BANJOS". The publisher and author suggest that the licensee contact PRS to ascertain the music publisher and contact such music publisher to license or acquire permission for performance of the song. If a licence or permission is unattainable for "CHIRPY CHIRPY CHEEP CHEEP" or "DUELING BANJOS", the licensee may not use the song in SOME MOTHERS DO 'AVE 'EM but should create an original composition in a similar style or use a similar song in the public domain. For further information, please see Music Use Note on page iii.

I'd creep over to you, I'd put my arms round you and I'd whisper into your ear: what's that funny smell?

BETTY. What?

> *(There is a loud bang from the kitchen as the record player automatically plays a song in the style of* ["GET DOWN"] *by Gilbert O'Sullivan.*)*

> *(They rush into the smoky kitchen.)*

FRANK. Oh no! It's the baking tray.

BETTY. The baking tray?

FRANK. *(Lifting the baking tray with a hole in it.)* Burnt straight through it. Oh! Ow! Ooh!

BETTY. Careful you'll burn your hands!

> *(She runs back to stop the record player.)*

Why was the gas on under the tray?

FRANK. *(Pointing at the recipe book.)* That's what it said: "Preheat it, before placing the tray in the oven".

BETTY. Preheat the *oven,* not the tray!

FRANK. Well how was I supposed to know? Fanny Cradock wasn't very clear with her instructions.

BETTY. Quick put your hands under the tap.

> *(The tap squirts all over* FRANK.*)*

---

* A licence to produce SOME MOTHERS DO 'AVE 'EM does not include a performance licence for "GET DOWN". The publisher and author suggest that the licensee contact PRS to ascertain the music publisher and contact such music publisher to license or acquire permission for performance of the song. If a licence or permission is unattainable for "GET DOWN", the licensee may not use the song in SOME MOTHERS DO 'AVE 'EM but should create an original composition in a similar style or use a similar song in the public domain. For further information, please see Music Use Note on page iii.

FRANK. Oh now look what's happened.

BETTY. I've been saying we should get someone to look at that!

FRANK. I'm getting to it, I'm getting to it. I'll put it on the list.

BETTY. No I mean someone qualified!

FRANK. *(Stopping.)* Qualified? Who made the front door may I ask? And the doorbell?

(The doorbell rings…)

– *Which* is still going strong if my ears don't deceive me.

(… But doesn't stop. He smacks the wall by the front door and the bell stops. He continues upstairs to take his jacket off.)

"Qualified" indeed. I'd like to know what this house'd be like if it wasn't for my toolbox.

(The shelf at the top of the stairs (holding a box of roller skates) drops at one end. **FRANK** *stops the skates from falling off just in time, and pushes the dropped edge of the shelf back up to its original height. It happens to hold.)*

BETTY. *(Under her breath.)* So would I.

*(***BETTY** *opens the door and sees a letter on the front step.)*

Oh.

(She picks it up and as **FRANK** *comes back downstairs,* **BETTY** *hands him the letter.)*

A LETTER FOR FRANK

Frank. It's a letter for you. Listen, I'm not faulting your efforts, you know I'm grateful for all your help around the house. I was only thinking that, well, we'd want to make sure everything was safe, wouldn't we? If we had anyone *else* around the house, Frank.

(**FRANK** *is reading the letter. Beat.*)

Frank?

FRANK. *(Quietly fearful.)* Betty.

BETTY. Yes Frank?

FRANK. Betty.

BETTY. I'm *here* Frank.

FRANK. I got a letter, Betty.

BETTY. Yes?

FRANK. From The BBC. I'm excited Betty.

BETTY. What does it say?

FRANK. You remember when we sat and watched the television together?

BETTY. Before you broke it, yes.

FRANK. And you remember that the BBC wanted entries for that new series.

BETTY. *Stars of Tomorrow?* Yes?

FRANK. Well Mr Mogford heard me talking about my act, and he sent my name in.

BETTY. Mr Mogford?

FRANK. From the DIY shop.

BETTY. What?

FRANK. I'm his best customer.

BETTY. Has he ever actually seen your act?

FRANK. *(Amazed by Mr Mogford's generosity.)* No he's never seen my DIY either! But I told him all about it, you see, and now the BBC have written to me in *writing*. I am the chosen one. And now their Head of Entertainment, Mr Terence S. Luscombe, wants to come here to meet me in person.

BETTY. Come *here*?

FRANK. *(Proud.)* "I would like to visit you at your home, if I may, outside of working hours..." Oh Betty! The BBC are prepared to visit outside my working hours!

BETTY. They can come anytime then. I'll put the kettle on.

FRANK. Oh no Betty, no-no-no, I think this calls for something a little stronger, don't you? I think we could open a bottle of the '64.

BETTY. The '64?

FRANK. Mother's homemade wine.

> (**BETTY** *goes to the cupboard to take out a bottle.*)

Oh Betty, this is the life. I've never been chosen to do anything before.

BETTY. Rhubarb or Prune?

FRANK. Definitely Rhubarb. '64 was a bad year for Prunes.

BETTY. *(Looking at the bottle.)* I'm sure it wasn't this colour last year.

FRANK. *(Shaking it all up.)* Oh no all the goodness has gone to the bottom.

BETTY. Don't shake it, Frank.

FRANK. This could be the making of us. With this news, Mr Worthington's bound to invest and all our problems will be solved. Just think, I could be in the Radio

Times. "Family man F W Spencer: Undiscovered Exhibitionist".

BETTY. Yes. And Frank, talking of family, I've got some news too.

FRANK. Your mother's not coming to live with us is she?

BETTY. You know I told you I was at the dentist's this afternoon?

FRANK. Of course, how did you get on? Will you have to have anything taken out?

BETTY. *Well...*

FRANK. *(Concerned.)* What's the matter?

BETTY. *(Re: the bottle.)* Could you put that down? Just for now?

FRANK. *(Putting it back in the cupboard.)* Oh yes. Better let it simmer down a bit.

BETTY. I tried to talk to you earlier, Frank.

FRANK. Any time, Betty, any time. As my mother always said, "A trouble shared is a trouble doubled".

BETTY. You promise you won't be too shocked?

FRANK. Shocked? "Shocke'" she says to her loving husband. If today's taught me a lesson, Betty, it's to be prepared for anything.

> *(Bang. The wine explodes (in the cupboard) and sprays out. The record player plays a song in the style of* **["TIE A YELLOW RIBBON**

ROUND THE OLE OAK TREE"] *by Dawn and Tony Orlando.*)*

(**BETTY** *stops the record.*)

BETTY. I told you that wine was unsafe!

> *(The next door neighbour bangs on the wall, and the picture of Jesus drops.)*

FRANK. Stop banging on my wall, Mr Rogers! You nearly defaced the Son of God.

BETTY. Don't lose your temper, Frank.

FRANK. *(Hanging the picture back up.)* He's got no patience, no patience at all! *(At the wall.)* I didn't know it was a bad year for rhubarb *too*!

BETTY. Don't spoil things now, Frank.

FRANK. He's been nothing but difficult ever since he had his hip done. Knocking off the Messiah at teatime. Rude man!

> *(The lamp by the door flickers.* **FRANK** *smacks the wall (the other side of the door) and it stops.)*

BETTY. So when's he coming, this Mr Luscombe?

FRANK. "We would like to visit you, at 8pm, on the 12th of April. Please be prepared to demonstrate"—

BETTY. The 12th of April? Frank! That's today!

FRANK. Today?! They *are* keen.

BETTY. *(Looking at the envelope.)* But the post-mark says the 20th of March. The postman must have delivered it next door whilst Mr Rogers was in hospital.

FRANK. Oh that's the third time that's happened! Why doesn't he deliver them here?

BETTY. We haven't got a letter box.

FRANK. I can't do everything at once, I'll put it on the list.

BETTY. You should have thought about it when you made the front door.

FRANK. I did. But the cat did a widdle on the blue prints.

BETTY. Wait if they're saying 8pm, they'll arrive when Mum and Mr Worthington are here.

FRANK. Better hold off on the prunes for now then.

BETTY. Do you think *I* better do the cooking, Frank? You've already got a lot to deal with.

FRANK. No-no-no, Betty, that's what they want to see! Me, Frank, cooking the meal, entertaining the guests: a dick of all trades. *(Heading upstairs.)* Now, now, now, first things first, where's my wedding suit?

BETTY. *(Pointing at the cupboard under the stairs.)* Your wedding suit?! Packed away under the stairs, why?

FRANK. *(Dashing down to the cupboard.)* It's a special occasion.

BETTY. *(Clearly anxious.)* Frank! Wait! Please!

　　　(Beat.)

FRANK. What is it? Everything all right?

BETTY. If we're going to have a full house this evening, I need to talk to you first.

(*Beat.*)

FRANK. (*Sheepish.*) Is it about the letter box?

BETTY. No, it's not about the letter box.

FRANK. Mr Lindbergh? I'll take him outside before they arrive.

BETTY. Will you come and sit down, Frank?

(*He does so, apprehensively.*)

Frank, there's going to be an addition to our family.

FRANK. How do you mean?

BETTY. We're going to hear the pitter-patter of tiny little feet.

(*Beat.*)

FRANK. Oh no-no-no, Betty, I'm not having another cat in this house.

(*The phone rings.*)

That'll be the phone.

(*The kitchen timer rings.*)

That'll be the timer. I'll deal with the timer, you deal with the phone.

(**FRANK** *takes the Wendy house out via the back door.*)

Sorry, Mr Lindbergh, we're expecting guests.

(*He then heads back into the kitchen to continue cooking.*)

Another cat! (*He tuts.*)

BETTY. Grays-Thurrock-five-double-six-seven-o? ... Oh hello Father O'Hara, everything all right? ... Oh no how awful! *(Away from phone.)* Frank! *(To phone.)* Well come and get ready here, you can join us for dinner... Yes of course... *(To phone.)* Frank!

(**FRANK**'s *head pops through the hatch.)*

FRANK. Yes m'lady?

BETTY. Father O'Hara's got a broken boiler.

FRANK. I'll put it on the list.

(**FRANK** *disappears.)*

BETTY. No I mean... *(To the phone.)* Yes, it's the least we can do... All right, see you shortly. Bye.

(Phone down.)

NOW WHAT'VE I GOT?

Father O'Hara's going to join us after all, Frank. I hope that's all right?

FRANK. *(Entering the living room with two spare chairs.)* Dinner for five coming up.

BETTY. What are you cooking?

FRANK. Beef!

BETTY. Beef? That'll take ages. They're arriving at half past.

FRANK. It's all right. It's only a bit of mince. "Fanny Cradock's finest'"

BETTY. All right then. You will try and get this right, won't you?

FRANK. Excuse me Betty. I always try.

BETTY. I know you do, but –

FRANK. *No one* could be more trying than me.

(**FRANK** *moves a dining chair and the leg falls off.*)

Oh no. Oh no no no. Oh no no no no no... oh no.

(*He slowly looks at* **BETTY** *holding the leg. He tuts.* **FRANK** *places it under the cushion.*)

Now, we've got your mother and Mr Worthington from the Bank, they can sit on the dining chairs, you and Father O'Hara, you can sit on the spare chairs, that'll work well. Now that leaves me with no chair, but I tell you what, stick a cushion on my magic case and I'll perch on the top.

BETTY. Are you sure?

FRANK. Yes, it'll be the most comfortable of the lot.

(*As he grabs the case he rips a piece of the wallpaper behind it.*)

Oh no. Oh no no no. Oh no no no no no... oh no.

(*He slowly looks at* **BETTY** *holding the wallpaper. He tuts.*)

BETTY. What is it?

FRANK. It's all right I can cover it over before the BBC arrive, they'll be none the wiser. Betty, give me the poster of Engelbert.

(**BETTY** *takes the frame off the wall, revealing an exposed hole in the plaster.*)

BETTY. Oh Frank – look!

FRANK. Oh I forgot about that one. I know, I can use the wallpaper from behind Brucie.

(**FRANK** *goes to move the Bruce Forsyth poster but rips the poster itself.*)

BETTY. Oh Frank!

FRANK. Sorry Brucie.

BETTY. What will the BBC say?

FRANK. It's all right don't worry. Now what have I got? Wallpaper torn twice. One good framed poster of Engelbert, one _torn_ _un_framed poster of *Brucie*. I tell you what – we'll put torn Brucie by the back door *(Which he does.)* and I'll take him out in the morning. _Now_ what've I got? One good framed poster of Engelbert and wallpaper torn twice. But if I move Engelbert over towards the door, we'll cover the first hole completely and this bit will be spare.

BETTY. What will you do with the bit that's spare?

FRANK. *(Doing it.)* Put it by the back door and take it out in the morning. _Now_ what've I got? One hole and one good magic case. But I also have good shelves covering a good wall, so I can put the good shelves over the good hole. That will be better all round, because with the good shelves over the good hole, the good hole will be nearer the good wall.

BETTY. How can the good hole be nearer the good wall?

FRANK. Good point. But the hole _will_ have the good shelves covering it.

BETTY. But what about this wall here? When you move the shelves up there...

FRANK. ... There will of course be a few feet of bare wall down here, so what I shall do is move the sofa from there to cover the good bare wall down here.

BETTY. But what about the torn paper?

FRANK. The torn paper's going out with torn Brucie.

BETTY. In the morning?

FRANK. In the morning.

(**FRANK** *moves the shelves.*)

BETTY. I don't want you messing up the house, Frank.

FRANK. I'm not messing it up, I'm just making a few adjustments.

BETTY. But how long is this going to take?

FRANK. Be patient, Betty. Rome wasn't burnt in a day. (*Putting the shelves half way up the stairs to cover the Engelbert poster.*) Now let's pop this up here.

BETTY. Be careful, Frank.

FRANK. Don't be so negative Betty, it's just a little rearrange, that's all. Here we go –

(*The shelves won't stand up.*)

That won't do. That won't do. I know, I'll use the tissue box and wedge it underneath.

(*After two failed attempts,* **FRANK** *grabs the tissue box from the shelves and props up one end – it balances perfectly.*)

(*Both picking up the sofa.*) Now, sofa to the wall yes? Come on – bend your knees, legs apart.

(*The sofa legs drop off on* **BETTY**'*s side stage left.*)

BETTY. Oh Frank – Look!

FRANK. What is it?

BETTY. The legs have broken.

FRANK. Well hold on, hold on. I'll get something to wedge it.

I know – the tissue box. It'll be just the right size.

(*He heads to the tissue box which is taking the weight of the shelves.*)

BETTY. Frank you can't use the tissue box, it's propping up the – Frank!!!

> *(Without thinking,* **FRANK** *swipes the tissue box from under the shelves, but the shelves stay upright.)*

FRANK. See? Don't be so pissomestic!

> *(The phone rings.)*

That'll be the phone.

> *(The kitchen timer rings.)*

That'll be the timer.

> *(The doorbell rings.)*

That'll be the doorbell.

BETTY. Oh Frank!

> *(***BETTY*** *panics, but* **FRANK** *instructs her logically and efficiently.)*

FRANK. Hang on Betty, we can do this, we can do this. *(He picks up the phone.)* One moment please. *(He smacks and opens the door.)* One moment please. *(He closes the door.)*

Now, Father O'Hara can sit on the good spare chair _here_, and your mother can sit on the good spare chair _there_. Good _Mr Worthington_ can sit on the good _dining_ chair _here_, and _you_ can sit carefully on the _not_-so-good dining chair _there_.

Now if _you_ turn on the little lamp over here, and the _not_-so-little _bigger_ lamp just _there_, *(Heading into the kitchen.)* _I'll_ turn up the _oven_ through _here_ and reset the _timer_ up _there_.

(Heading back.) You turn on the little-*bigger little* lamp over there, and turn *off* the last lamp lit up there, then all that's left to say is *(He picks up the phone.)* "I'm sorry I think you have the wrong number", *(He disconnects the handset and throws it.)* pull that out, put it in the corner, take it out in the morning, put it on the list – and while I change into my wedding suit, you open the good front door. Thank you.

> *(FRANK shuts the cupboard door behind him.)*

> *(The doorbell rings again. BETTY smacks the wall and opens the front door, aware that FRANK can hear all of the following from the cupboard. MRS FISHER enters.)*

HELLO MUM

BETTY. Hello Mum.

MRS FISHER. There's my little girl!

BETTY. Hello Mum.

MRS FISHER. Hello darling.

BETTY. Sorry for the wait –

MRS FISHER. I was beginning to think you'd moved out; one lives in hope.

BETTY. Sorry Mum.

MRS FISHER. But one surprise is enough for today. Congratulations, darling!

BETTY. *(Whilst signaling to stop talking.)* Oh yes!

MRS FISHER. I thought the day would never dawn.

BETTY. *(Covering.)* It's wonderful for Frank isn't it.

MRS FISHER. What?

BETTY. It's terrific news for *Frank*.

MRS FISHER. Well yes, none of my friends thought he had it in him.

BETTY. Well that's *magic* for you.

MRS FISHER. Eh?

FRANK. *(From cupboard.)* Hello Mrs Fisher.

MRS FISHER. *(Impulsively snappy.)* What's that! Hello?!

FRANK. It's Frank.

MRS FISHER. *(Looking for him.)* Frank?

FRANK. Your son-in-law.

MRS FISHER. *(To* **BETTY.***)* Where is he?

BETTY. Don't panic, Mum, he's in the cupboard.

MRS FISHER. The cupboard?

> (**BETTY** *takes* **MRS FISHER** *away from the cupboard.)*

FRANK. Don't worry Mrs Fisher, I'll be out soon.

> (**FRANK** *shuts the cupboard door again.)*

MRS FISHER. Why's he in the cupboard?

BETTY. *(Whispering.)* Sshh. He doesn't know.

MRS FISHER. *(Whispering.)* He doesn't know why he's in the cupboard?

BETTY. *(Whispering.)* The *news* – I haven't told him yet.

MRS FISHER. *(Whispering.)* Why not? It is *his* isn't it?

BETTY. *(Whispering.)* Mum! I tried telling him but he wouldn't listen.

MRS FISHER. *(Whispering.)* So you locked him in the cupboard?

BETTY. *(Whispering.)* No –

FRANK. What are you two whispering about?

BETTY. *(Full voice again.)* I thought Mr Worthington was picking you up, Mum?

MRS FISHER. He's just parking the car – no spaces outside so he dropped me at the front gate. Oh wait 'til you meet him Betty, he's given me a whole new lease of life. And with his rich Scottish tones, he only has to say "Goodnight" to me and I want to toss the caber.

BETTY. *(To get* **MRS FISHER** *to come upstairs.)* Mum, I want to put something a bit smarter on, would you come and help me choose something? We'll leave the door open for Mr Worthington.

> *(Leaving the front door ajar, they head upstairs.)*

MRS FISHER. Yes darling, of course.

> *(On the way up.)*

Dressing for dinner now are we? If I'd known I'd have made more of an effort.

> (**FRANK** *waves a pair of creased, light blue trousers out of the cupboard.)*

FRANK. Betty? My trousers are all creased, you couldn't give 'em a quick iron could you? *(Head popping out of the cupboard.)* Betty? If you want something doing, you better do it yourself. Ironing board.

> *(He heads into the kitchen with the ironing board, dressed in socks, y-fronts and a ruffled, dress shirt – but no trousers.)*

> *(He tries, in vain, to put the ironing board up. Eventually he gives up and lays it flat across the kitchen sink and work top.)*

Iron.

> (*He goes to take the iron from on top of the cupboard, and a small bit of porridge spills from the box next to the iron.*)

Oh. Mind the porridge.

Ooh. Now, trousers.

HELLO MR WORTHINGTON

> (*Looking around for the trousers, he realises that he's left them in the cupboard. As he re-enters the living room,* **MR WORTHINGTON** *enters through the front door.*)

MR WORTHINGTON. Hello?

> (**FRANK** *dashes back into the kitchen and shuts the door quickly.*)

> (*Heading towards the kitchen.*)

Anybody in?

> (**FRANK** *is looking for some trousers around the ironing board and the cupboards.*)

> (**MR WORTHINGTON** *knocks on the kitchen door and goes to open it.*)

Knock knock, anyone at home?

FRANK. (*Bursting through the hatch.*) Good evening, Mr Worthington... Frank Spencer. Undiscovered Exhibitionist.

MR WORTHINGTON. Hello Frank. David Worthington.

> (*They shake hands.*)

FRANK. Nice to meet you, Mr Worthington.

MR WORTHINGTON. Please, call me David. I *wondered* who was in the kitchen.

FRANK. Yes *I'm* in charge tonight.

MR WORTHINGTON. Very impressive!

FRANK. I was an apprentice chef at the Fleece Hotel.

MR WORTHINGTON. Really?

FRANK. Before it burnt down of course.

MR WORTHINGTON. Were you there when the fire started?

FRANK. I was the *only* one there when the fire started.

> *(Signaling to the coat hooks.)*

Do take your hat and coat off. I'll be round in a minute.

MR WORTHINGTON. Thank you.

> *(**FRANK** discovers a pair of brown trousers on the airer.)*

FRANK. *(Under breath.)* Aha.

> *(During the following, **FRANK** races to put them on and enter the living room but doesn't realise they're actually a brown skirt of **BETTY***'s.)*

> *(At the last second he pushes the skirt through his legs before **MR WORTHINGTON** turns round, so it looks like he's wearing a pair of tight, brown trousers.)*

MR WORTHINGTON. *(Putting his hat and coat by the door.)* Well it's very good of you to include me at such short notice. A little impromptu invite from Barbara was rather a nice surprise and I believe con...

> *(Catches sight of **FRANK**.)*

I believe congratulations are in order.

FRANK. *(Re: the BBC. Surprised and confused.)* Oh... You know do you?

MR WORTHINGTON. Yes, Barbara told me on the way here. Capital news for both of you.

FRANK. Well thank you. I only found out ten minutes ago. Betty must have told her mother on the phone. Doesn't news travel fast when you're having fun!

MR WORTHINGTON. And Barbara tells me this is your first – that's doubly exciting.

FRANK. Oh yes, first time indeed – and a complete surprise. *(A secret.)* To be honest, if I hadn't spoken to Mr Mogford, I wouldn't have stood a chance.

MR WORTHINGTON. Mr Mogford?

FRANK. He's my supplier.

MR WORTHINGTON. I see.

FRANK. Oh no, Mr Worthington, it's all very good stuff – he gets it from overseas I think. It used to be a little flimsy in this house, but since I went to Mr Mogford, *(Taps on the banister.)* solid as a rock. If you tip me the wink, I'll get you a special deal.

MR WORTHINGTON. *(Changing the subject.)* And how's Betty doing? How's she feeling?

FRANK. A little nervous I think, and she's not been feeling herself lately, hence why I'm in the kitchen.

MR WORTHINGTON. Is there anything I can do to help? Shall I come round?

FRANK. *(Backing in to the kitchen, signaling to the 3-legged chair.)* No no! You make yourself at home, Mr Worthington. Please, take a seat, and take the floor, off your feet.

MR WORTHINGTON. If you say so.

> (**MR WORTHINGTON** *goes to sit on the three-legged chair.*)

FRANK. (*Suddenly.*) But not there please! I'd prefer you to sit on another chair if you don't mind. It's a better view.

MR WORTHINGTON. Right.

> (**MR WORTHINGTON** *goes to sit on the other chairs, one by one.*)

FRANK. No not that one... No not that one... That one. Now sit back and relax, you'll soon discover that I have what it takes to take what you have.

> (*He exits to the kitchen.* **MRS FISHER** *hurries downstairs into the living room.*)

MRS FISHER. Sorry David, I'll be down in a minute, Betty just wanted a bit of fashion advice, you know. Are you all right staying here for a moment?

MR WORTHINGTON. I daren't move.

MRS FISHER. I won't leave you here long, don't worry.

> (*Whispering.*)

Oh and if you wouldn't mind, don't talk about it with Frank, will you?

MR WORTHINGTON. What do you mean?

MRS FISHER. (*Whispering.*) Don't mention anything about the baby. We're not supposed to know.

MR WORTHINGTON. (*Whispering.*) Why not?

MRS FISHER. (*Whispering.*) Frank doesn't know yet.

MR WORTHINGTON. (*Whispering.*) Yes he does he just mentioned it to me.

MRS FISHER. (*Whispering.*) He can't have done.

MR WORTHINGTON. *(Whispering.)* I'm pretty sure he did. Why would he *not* know?

MRS FISHER. *(Whispering.)* Precisely what *I* said.

BETTY. *(From upstairs.)* Mum?

MRS FISHER. *(Whispering.)* It's all a bit complicated but I'll explain later. As long as you're all right. We'll be down shortly.

MR WORTHINGTON. *(Whispering.)* Why are we whispering?

MRS FISHER. *(Whispering.)* He's in the cupboard.

FRANK'S NEW "VENTURE"

*(She rushes back upstairs. **FRANK** enters holding an autumnal tablecloth over his exposed legs. He sidles across the room.)*

FRANK. Mr Worthington, I wonder if I could talk to you about my personal assets, before the arrival of "you know what" – my financial situation if you were.

MR WORTHINGTON. Right, yes, well I suppose if you're going to be starting a new "venture", money's very important.

FRANK. Well precisely, I agree. I came very close to fifty thousand pounds last year.

MR WORTHINGTON. Fifty thousand pounds?!

FRANK. Yes.

MR WORTHINGTON. Well, well, well. That's incredible!

FRANK. Thank you. I was just one number out.

MR WORTHINGTON. What, you mean premium bonds?! That's your income?

FRANK. And I have a bit of savings left from when my mother died. As an only child I am the sole heir of the family.

MR WORTHINGTON. Look can I give you a hand with that tablecloth?

FRANK. It's all right, it's not heavy, I just don't want to crease it.

MR WORTHINGTON. *(Heading towards* FRANK.*)* ...Putting it on the table though, I'll give you a hand.

FRANK. No no please I don't need any help –

> *(Fearing that* MR WORTHINGTON *will expose him,* FRANK *flings the tablecloth across the table whilst sitting down himself. He also grabs the vase of flowers placing it on top of the cloth.* MR WORTHINGTON *still can't see* FRANK*'s exposed legs.)*

> *(Re: the vase.)*

This vase was presented to my father.

MR WORTHINGTON. Oh very nice. Chinese?

FRANK. No he was English. Same as me.

MR WORTHINGTON. Was it *made* by the Chinese?

FRANK. Oh possibly. He did give them a lot of business.

MR WORTHINGTON. Hong Kong stock?

FRANK. Pe-king Duck.

MR WORTHINGTON. Now then, I stopped at the off-licence on the way here.

FRANK. Oh thank you.

MR WORTHINGTON. I was quite surprised to find anything open actually, must be jolly convenient having somewhere like that on your doorstep.

(During the above, as **MR WORTHINGTON** *goes to the door for the bottle of wine,* **FRANK** *quickly grabs the bottle of prune wine.)*

FRANK. I've just got one out actually.

MR WORTHINGTON. Well keep this one for next time. Nothing special I'm afraid – it's a Dry Riesling.

FRANK. Oh nice. *(Referring to his own.)* Mine's a wet prune.

MR WORTHINGTON. Well there's a first time for everything eh? A couple of *glasses* and we'll be raring to go.

FRANK. Glasses? Mr Worthington, do you like my hatch?

MR WORTHINGTON. Your hatch?

*(**FRANK** points to the serving hatch.)*

Oh yes it's very nice.

FRANK. Installed it myself only last week. Swing hinges, swing doors. *(Pushing the doors.)* Rat a tat tat!

MR WORTHINGTON. Very neatly done. Must have been a big job.

FRANK. Oh yes.

MR WORTHINGTON. I'm surprised it's not structural in a house like this.

FRANK. Structural?

MR WORTHINGTON. The wall obviously isn't structural to the rest of the house. It's not a supporting wall.

FRANK. Oh, no-no it's not a supporting wall. Not since I put a hole in it.

MR WORTHINGTON. So it *is* structural?! Mr Spencer –

FRANK. Please, call me Frank.

MR WORTHINGTON. You can't cut a hole in a supporting wall. What about consent? Did you get approval?

FRANK. Oh yes. Betty loved the idea.

MR WORTHINGTON. Betty?! You can't get planning permission from your wife. You need an architect, and to submit forms to the council, and that's just –

FRANK. I think you misunderestimate me, Mr Worthington. I was an apprentice with Chandley Properties as a teenager.

I may not look the type but I've been around the bush. And I say that without fear of contraception.

MR WORTHINGTON. Goodness, I hadn't realised you'd worked in property.

FRANK. Yes. I only left due to unforeseen circumstances.

MR WORTHINGTON. What happened?

FRANK. I was sacked.

> *(Beat.)*

MR WORTHINGTON. *(Changing the subject.)* Isn't it time we had a drink?

FRANK. Drink.

MR WORTHINGTON. Yes.

FRANK. Drink.

MR WORTHINGTON. Those glasses won't fetch themselves.

FRANK. Glasses.

MR WORTHINGTON. Yes.

FRANK. Glasses.

MR WORTHINGTON. *(Heading towards the kitchen, nearly exposing* **FRANK.***)* Should *I* go perhaps?

FRANK. No don't move!

MR WORTHINGTON. What? Why not?

FRANK. *(Pretending to hear something.)* Because... of the... owl.

MR WORTHINGTON. What?

FRANK. The owl. Didn't you hear him? He must be waking up.

MR WORTHINGTON. The owl?

FRANK. Yes. If you close your eyes and listen, Mr Worthington, you'll just about hear him.

MR WORTHINGTON. Right. Very good.

> *(***MR WORTHINGTON*** *reluctantly shuts his eyes, whilst* **FRANK** *collects a couple of glasses from the kitchen.)*

FRANK. You must keep your eyes shut and block out the surroundings, then you will hear him.

MR WORTHINGTON. Right. Yes. Okay.

FRANK. *(Disappearing into the cupboard.)* No peeking now.

MR WORTHINGTON. What exactly am I listening for?

> *(***FRANK*** *starts making owl hooting noises.)*

Ah yes there it is.

> *(He opens his eyes.)*

Mr Spencer? Frank?

> *(He locates where the owl hooting is coming from and heads towards the cupboard. As he gets close, the noises stop mid-hoot. As* **MR WORTHINGTON** *knocks on the cupboard door, the doorbell rings,* **FRANK** *bursts out of the cupboard, fully dressed in a light blue*

morning suit, brown trousers and corsage. He marches past MR WORTHINGTON *to the front door.)*

FRANK. *(Pointing at them.)* Two glasses, raring to go.

(He smacks the wall to stop the doorbell and opens the front door.)

WELCOME BACK, FATHER O'HARA

Good evening, Father O'Hara. Do come in.

FATHER O'HARA. Good evening, Mr Spencer. It's very kind of you to help me out in my hour of need.

FRANK. Not at all, Father, not at all. Father O'Hara, this is Mr Worthington from the bank. Mr Worthington, this is Father O'Hara, from the church.

(He zips up his trousers.)

MR WORTHINGTON. Good evening, Father.

FATHER O'HARA. Hello.

MR WORTHINGTON. David Worthington.

FATHER O'HARA. Good evening, David.

FRANK. Father O'Hara wasn't invited, but he's having problems with his waterworks.

FATHER O'HARA. Well, I –

FRANK. And we're always happy to have you, Father. Particularly on a *special occasion* like this.

FATHER O'HARA. *(Re: the baby.)* Ahhh! Congratulations Mr Spencer!

FRANK. Oh you know as well?

FATHER O'HARA. *(Laughing.)* I'm sorry. I wasn't sure if *you* knew yet.

FRANK. Why would I *not* know? I am the man of the hour am I not? I am he.

MR WORTHINGTON. Exactly what I said to Barbara – she told me to keep it quiet just in case.

FRANK. Funny woman. Now drinks! Drinks! Without further ado. Poor Mr Worthington must be starched. *(To* **FATHER O'HARA**.*)* You'll have a glass of the '64 won't you, Father?

FATHER O'HARA. Oh, well, er, just a small one.

> (**FRANK** *pops the cork with a fart noise.*)

FRANK. That'll be the prunes. Two glasses coming right up.

FATHER O'HARA. To think we could have spent the whole evening trying to keep our mouths shut.

FRANK. *(Handing out the glasses of wine.)* We've not long known ourselves, and Betty still finds the time to call her mother and Father O'Hara. I hope the details are correct or by the time it reaches the rest of the parish, it'll be like a Chinese Whisker. Cheers!

FATHER O'HARA. Cheers.

MR WORTHINGTON. Whis*per*.

FRANK. *(Whispering.)* Cheers.

> (*They all take a sip of the wine.*)

MR WORTHINGTON & FATHER O'HARA. *(Approving.)* Mmm.

FRANK. Wait for it.

> (*The after-kick arrives, like raw horseradish up the nose.*)

MR WORTHINGTON & FATHER O'HARA. Oaagh!

FRANK. Got a bit of a zing to it. Let me take your coat, Father.

FATHER O'HARA. I think Mrs Spencer was a little apprehensive earlier about the whole thing – as one would expect of course.

FRANK. Imagine how *I'm* feeling.

FATHER O'HARA. The lord must be looking out for you both. Forgive me for saying so, Mr Spencer, but you've been waiting a long time for this.

FRANK. *(Touched.)* Thank you, Father, yes. Between you and me, when I started I didn't know what I was doing. So there's been a lot of leg work involved: often just changing my angles; giving it another shuffle; *(Trade secrets.)* but the thing that really gets 'em going... is all sleight of hand.

FATHER O'HARA. Please Mr Spencer, I don't think we need to know all the details.

FRANK. No, you're right, I shouldn't spoil it for you, Father. It must be more fun when you don't know how the magic happens.

FATHER O'HARA. Really Mr Spencer!

FRANK. "Abracadabra!" – "Where did that come from?"

MR WORTHINGTON. So when did you find out Frank?

FRANK. Only this evening. The letter was delivered next door you see.

FATHER O'HARA. The letter?

FRANK. Oh yes, it's all official.

MR WORTHINGTON. They don't tell you by post, do they?

FRANK. First class and all.

MR WORTHINGTON. Well I never.

FATHER O'HARA. Betty never mentioned a letter.

FRANK. Truth be told, gentlemen, it's got me all a little nervous.

MR WORTHINGTON. Well of course, these moments don't come around very often.

FRANK. I think it's the pressure, you know – there's no room for error.

MR WORTHINGTON. But the doctors will help you with any problems along the way.

FRANK. The doctors?! That's very kind Mr Worthington but I'm not *that* worried. No no, I'm determined to do this all by myself.

FATHER O'HARA. I'm not sure I follow.

FRANK. Well I'll have plenty of time to practise. And when the big day arrives, I will deliver!

FATHER O'HARA & MR WORTHINGTON. Deliver?

FRANK. Just you wait – if it's there for the taking, I'm gonna grab it with both hands.

FATHER O'HARA. But you're not qualified, Mr Spencer.

FRANK. You'd be surprised how few people are. And besides, I spent most of my teenage years practising on my mother.

> *(The kitchen timer rings.* **FRANK** *grabs the blue trousers from the cupboard.)*

Now if you'll excuse me gentlemen, "A woman's work is never done!"

> *(He goes into the kitchen, puts the trousers on the ironing board and takes his brown ones off.)*

MR WORTHINGTON. Good grief.

FATHER O'HARA. Dear me. The man's extraordinary.

MR WORTHINGTON. A self-taught midwife? When does he find time to go to work?

FATHER O'HARA. He doesn't go to work. He goes to *interviews*, but he never goes to work.

> (**FRANK** *holds a plate of hors d'oeuvres through the hatch.*)

FRANK. Gentlemen: can I interest you in one of my late mother's pickled apricots? Father, you'll do me the honours?

FATHER O'HARA. Thank you.

FRANK. And Mr Worthington, one she prepared earlier?

MR WORTHINGTON. I won't. Thank you.

FRANK. They're meant to be swallowed in one, Father.

> (**FRANK** *disappears.* **FATHER O'HARA** *swallows the apricot.*)

> (*From the kitchen.*)

Just take the stone out first.

> (**FATHER O'HARA** *begins choking on the apricot.*)

MR WORTHINGTON. For goodness sake. Mr Spencer!

FRANK. (*Through hatch.*) Yes, Mr Worthington?

MR WORTHINGTON. Father O'Hara. He's choking on the apricot.

FRANK. Choking on the – Oohh.

> (*Rushing through with no trousers.*)

It's all right Father, don't panic. I'm trained in the Heineken manoeuvre. Four very easy steps to remember. Now what are they? Step 1: Determine if the patient is definitely choking. Father O'Hara, are you definitely choking?

MR WORTHINGTON. Of course he's choking, do something!

FRANK. You're definitely choking, I'll move on to step 2. Step 2: Reassure the victim you are going to help them immediately. Father, I am going to help you immediately.

MR WORTHINGTON. Get on with it Frank! The poor man's fading fast. Barbara!

FRANK. All right Step 3 – I can't remember step 3 – Step 4: stand where you are Father. I've done this before – just relax, and pretend you're the scout master.

> (**FRANK** *performs the Heimlich manoeuvre on* **FATHER O'HARA,** *which starts the record player, with a song in the style of* ["**DUELING BANJOS**"] *by Eric Weissberg and Steve Mandell.**)

That's it father. And ooh! And ooh! And yes Father! Yes Father! Hold on to the chair.

HOW DID YOU KNOW?

> (**FRANK** *goes double time with* **FATHER O'HARA. MRS FISHER** *and* **BETTY** *arrive at the top of the stairs.*)

---

* A licence to produce SOME MOTHERS DO 'AVE 'EM does not include a performance licence for "DUELING BANJOS". The publisher and author suggest that the licensee contact PRS to ascertain the music publisher and contact such music publisher to license or acquire permission for performance of the song. If a licence or permission is unattainable for "DUELING BANJOS", the licensee may not use the song in SOME MOTHERS DO 'AVE 'EM but should create an original composition in a similar style or use a similar song in the public domain. For further information, please see Music Use Note on page iii.

> (*Eventually the apricot flies out of* **FATHER O'HARA***'s mouth and* **MR WORTHINGTON** *catches it.*)

> (**FRANK** *stops the music.*)

I learnt that at the Jamboree. (*Scouts salute.*) I *will* do my best. (*Passing him his wine glass.*) Dyb, dyb, dyb, dub, dub, dub, where's Akela? In the pub! There you go father.

> (**FATHER O'HARA** *takes a sip of wine.*)

Wait for it.

FATHER O'HARA. Oaagh!

FRANK. Oh dear. Here have a seat.

> (**FRANK** *brings the three legged chair which gives way as* **FATHER O'HARA** *sits on it.*)

FATHER O'HARA. Agh!

FRANK. Oh no, Father, that's Betty's chair. Let's get you up.

MR WORTHINGTON. (*Losing it.*) Leave the man alone, for God's sake! Just give him some space. Please!

MRS FISHER. Everything all right David?

MR WORTHINGTON. If it's not a pickled apricot, it's a three legged chair or a glass of prune wine.

MRS FISHER. How many have you had?

> (**BETTY** *gets* **FATHER O'HARA** *on to another chair.*)

BETTY. Here, Father.

FRANK. I was trying to help, that's all.

BETTY. I'm sure it was just a misunderstanding.

MRS FISHER. I hope it *was* a misunderstanding.

FRANK. When I did it for the cubs, they gave me a Curly Wurly.

(Beat.)

MR WORTHINGTON. I'm sure you were just trying to help.

BETTY. Listen, I'll clear it up, you go and sort yourself out, Frank. If you serve up dinner now we'll be all done and dusted by the time they arrive.

FRANK. Righto.

MR WORTHINGTON. Who else is coming?

MRS FISHER. *(Re: the BBC.)* Oh yes, Congratulations Frank.

FRANK. *(Before entering the kitchen.)* Thank you.

MRS FISHER. Haven't you told David the good news?

MR WORTHINGTON. *(Re: the baby.)* Well he...

BETTY. Frank's had some special news this evening.

MR WORTHINGTON. Yes I ...

FRANK. We've already set the ball rolling, haven't we, Mr Worthington?

MR WORTHINGTON. Well we... yes – yes it's splendid news, splendid! *(To MRS FISHER.)* Sorry, I –

MRS FISHER. Betty told me upstairs.

MR WORTHINGTON. Oh, I see. Oh right I'm with you now.

FRANK. *(To MRS FISHER, re: the BBC.)* But that's odd... I thought you knew *already*?

MRS FISHER. Not until just now.

BETTY. *(Re: the BBC.)* You didn't mind me telling Mum did you, Frank?

FRANK. No no. But you *must* have known, otherwise how did *you* know, Mr Worthington?

MR WORTHINGTON. Well we "didn't", did we?

MRS FISHER. No, not at all.

FRANK. But you *did* though.

MRS FISHER. No we didn't.

MR WORTHINGTON. Well we *did*, but we "didn't" For *although* we did, we didn't know if *Frank* did so we didn't want to *say* we did in case he *didn't* did we?

MRS FISHER. Didn't *what*?

MR WORTHINGTON. Didn't *know*.

MRS FISHER. Know *what*?

MR WORTHINGTON. Know *this*.

MRS FISHER. Know *what*?

MR WORTHINGTON. Well *this*.

MRS FISHER. Oh right.

MR WORTHINGTON. Yes?

MRS FISHER. Right.

MR WORTHINGTON. Yes?

MRS FISHER. Right.

BETTY. Wait a minute, Mum, we are talking about the *same thing* here aren't we?

MRS FISHER. I *think* we are.

MR WORTHINGTON. *I* think we are.

FATHER O'HARA. I don't know *what* to think.

BETTY. Frank, you tell us what *you* were talking about then and we can get back on track.

FRANK. Well the letter of course.

MRS FISHER. That's right!

MR WORTHINGTON. That's right!

BETTY. That's right!

FATHER O'HARA. That's right!

FRANK. I really love your tiger light?

> *(They all look at* **FRANK.***)*

FATHER O'HARA. So you *did* know then?

MRS FISHER. Oh please, I can't bear it. I need a drink.

MR WORTHINGTON. I need a cigarette.

FRANK. I need trousers.

MRS FISHER. Cheers.

> *(***MRS FISHER** *drinks some wine.)*

Mmm.

MR WORTHINGTON, FATHER O'HARA & FRANK. Wait for it...

MRS FISHER. *(Aftertaste is even better.)* Mmm!

> *(The kitchen timer rings.)*

FRANK. Ladies and Gentlemen: It's time!

ALL. *(Positive.)* Ah!

FRANK. Time to put the veg on!

ALL. *(Disappointed.)* Oh.

MRS FISHER. What's on the menu, Frank?

FRANK. Beef!

ALL. *(Positive.)* Ah!

FRANK. Beef "à la Fanny!"

ALL. *(Fearful.)* Ooh!

> (**FRANK** *goes into the kitchen and puts his trousers on.*)

BETTY. How are you feeling, Father?

FATHER O'HARA. Much better thank you, yes. Bit of a shock you know, but I'll be right as rain in a moment.

BETTY. Can I get you anything?

FATHER O'HARA. No thank you.

A SMALL LOAN FOR ME

> (**FRANK** *comes back in. He and* **BETTY** *prepare the table for a business conversation.*)

FRANK. Mr Worthington, whilst we wait for the final preparations in the kitchen, I'd be internally grateful if I could talk to you about my business prepositions, for which, I suspect, I may garden your interest. The thing is, I know that Worthington & Sons lend people money, and I was wondering if you could arrange a small loan for me?

MR WORTHINGTON. *(Suddenly taken aback, and on best behaviour to his customer.)* A loan?

FRANK. Yes!

MR WORTHINGTON. *(Sitting down.)* Oh, I am terribly sorry, Mr Spencer. I didn't realise you had interests in Worthington & Sons.

FRANK. I realise I may not compete with your effluent customers, but as my mother always said, "Half a loaf is better than one".

MR WORTHINGTON. *(Taking out a notebook.)* Well, Mr Spencer, you'll understand we have very particular criteria for whom we lend money to –

FRANK. As 'tis your provocative.

MR WORTHINGTON. – So may I start by asking you some personal questions?

FRANK. Like what?

MR WORTHINGTON. Well, for example, what is your occupation?

FRANK. No.

MR WORTHINGTON. No?

FRANK. My occupation. No. I'm in-between jobs.

MR WORTHINGTON. I see, right, and which jobs are you in-between?

FRANK. My last one and my next one.

BETTY. What was your *last* job, Frank?

FRANK. Ah I was a train guard.

MR WORTHINGTON. A train guard, good, good. Now how many years did you do that? Two, three?

FRANK. Five.

MR WORTHINGTON. Five years.

FRANK. Days.

MR WORTHINGTON. Five *days*?!

FRANK. I kept forgetting to open the doors.

BETTY. *(For* **MR WORTHINGTON.***)* Oh but he was a very good guard, wasn't he Mum? No-one fell as they got off the train.

MRS FISHER. No-one got off at all.

MR WORTHINGTON. Let's try something else. Do you have any qualifications?

FRANK. One.

MR WORTHINGTON. English? Maths?

FRANK. Breaststroke. Twenty five yards.

FATHER O'HARA. But you went to school, Frank.

FRANK. Oh yes, yes.

MR WORTHINGTON. And how old were you when you started school? Four, five?

FRANK. Ten.

MR WORTHINGTON. Ten?! Good god.

FRANK. It was a long journey. And there weren't any buses.

MR WORTHINGTON. How old were you when you left?

FRANK. About 11.

MR WORTHINGTON. You only spent a year at school?

FRANK. Yes but my mother still took me in the Summer holidays. So I wouldn't get bullied.

MR WORTHINGTON. *(Giving up.)* Mr Spencer, I'm afraid I ...

> *(Everyone simultaneously pleads with* **MR WORTHINGTON.***)*

BETTY.	MRS FISHER.	FATHER O'HARA
Mr Worthington, please, Frank's been very unlucky recently and I –	– Oh David, there must be some way you can help, for me at least –	Oh dear now, I'm sure even a little bit of help would make a big difference –

MR WORTHINGTON. Look before we'd issue a loan, to *any* of our clients, firstly we would need the names of two referees.

FRANK. I'm not a football fan.

MR WORTHINGTON. For a *reference*: professionals who could vouch for you, and *secondly*, we'd need you to put up some form of security – your house for instance.

FRANK. Ah yes, yes!

MR WORTHINGTON. Right, do you know its current value?

FRANK. Not off-hand no. But I could ask the landlord.

MR WORTHINGTON. The landlord?!

BETTY. Mr Worthington is asking if we are the *owners* of this house.

FRANK. Ah well I wouldn't put it *quite* like that.

MR WORTHINGTON. How *would* you put it?

FRANK. We are *not* the owners of this house.

FATHER O'HARA. But the landlord could give him a *reference*.

MR WORTHINGTON. True, true – he must be happy after you saved him all this money.

FRANK. He will be when I tell him.

MR WORTHINGTON. He doesn't know?! You can't go knocking hatches through without permission from the landlord. If he finds out, he'll have you paying for the damage. That's if he doesn't take you to court.

BETTY. Court?

MRS FISHER. Oh my God!

FRANK. Oohh.

FATHER O'HARA. Goodness me.

MRS FISHER. *(Having blasphemed.)* Sorry Father.

FRANK. Wait a minute I know! My psychiatrist could give me a reference.

MR WORTHINGTON. Your psychiatrist? Are you having treatment?

FRANK. No no no that's all finished now. I only went to him because I thought I was a failure.

MR WORTHINGTON. And what did he say?

FRANK. He thought I was too.

MR WORTHINGTON. *(Standing.)* Good evening, Mr Spencer.

FRANK. You're leaving?

MR WORTHINGTON. What does it look like? Come on, Barbara.

BETTY. What about dinner, Mr Worthington?

MRS FISHER. It's nearly ready isn't it, Frank?

MR WORTHINGTON. Well if it's anything like the pickled apricots – or the wine, which is positively toxic –

FRANK. You leave my mother out of this.

MR WORTHINGTON. What?

BETTY. Frank!?

FRANK. It's got nothing to do with her.

MR WORTHINGTON. I didn't say anything about your mother.

FRANK. Yes you did – you insulted her wine.

MR WORTHINGTON. I didn't know it *was* her wine.

MRS FISHER. I rather *like* the wine.

MR WORTHINGTON. Let me be very clear. I have no problems with your mother, I have never even *met* your mother. And although it would be nice to help all those in need, I'm quite frankly surprised we gave you an account in the first place.

FRANK. You didn't.

MR WORTHINGTON. What?

FRANK. But if you *do* lend me the money, I *will* open an account with you.

MR WORTHINGTON. Mr Spencer. This conversation is over. Good evening.

FRANK. I could put you in the black.

MR WORTHINGTON. You'd put me in a bloody home.

FRANK. Oooh!

MR WORTHINGTON. Barbara, where's your coat?

MRS FISHER. I did warn you.

BETTY. Mum!

FRANK. Swearing in my living room.

BETTY. Mum, please don't go.

FRANK. My psychiatrist never swore.

MR WORTHINGTON. Oh for goodness sake.

FRANK. Even when he strangled me. We've got to start somewhere.

MR WORTHINGTON. You've no money, no account, no house and no job.

FRANK. That doesn't tell you everything.

MR WORTHINGTON. You've made illegal alterations to a house that doesn't belong to you, your referee is a psychiatrist who thinks you're a failure, and your only source of income is child benefit from a baby that hasn't been born yet.

(The ladies gasp. **FRANK** *looks at* **BETTY.***)*

MRS FISHER. Oh no.

MR WORTHINGTON. What?

MRS FISHER. What did you go and say that for?

MR WORTHINGTON. What do you mean?

MRS FISHER. Oh no.

FATHER O'HARA. I don't think I follow.

FRANK. Betty? What's he saying?

BETTY. It's true Frank, I'm so sorry, I tried to tell you earlier, I really did. I'm going to have a baby.

MR WORTHINGTON. What? He didn't know? You're not telling me *I* – But what on earth have we been talking about?

MRS FISHER. His magic, David. We never even mentioned the baby.

MR WORTHINGTON. His magic?

MRS FISHER. He's trying to become a magician. Come on I'll explain outside.

MR WORTHINGTON. A Magician? Mr Spencer? Oh bloody hell!

> (**MRS FISHER** *ushers* **MR WORTHINGTON** *outside.*)

MRS FISHER. I thought I made it clear we weren't supposed to know. Come on.

MR WORTHINGTON. Yes but then he told us he – Oh bloody hell!

> (*They leave.*)

FATHER O'HARA. I'll go and put the kettle on.

> (*He goes into the kitchen.*)

SAY SOMETHING, FRANK

BETTY. Please say something, Frank.

FRANK. Well you might have asked me first.

BETTY. I thought you'd be pleased.

FRANK. That's all right Betty – if you've made up your mind. I won't stand in your way. It's just that I don't like you doing things behind my back.

BETTY. What are you talking about?

FRANK. I know what you're like. You'll bring it home and look after it, you'll grow fond of it. And then one day the mother'll come back and take it home again. And I don't want you getting upset.

BETTY. I'm not talking about someone else's baby. It's *our* baby. I'm its mother.

FRANK. You're its... you mean... I'm its...

BETTY. That's right.

(Beginning to faint.)

FRANK. ... Oooh.

BETTY. Steady, Frank.

FRANK. Are you sure?

BETTY. Yes. Quite sure. I had to have an appointment this afternoon before I knew for certain. That's why I told you I'd been to the dentist.

FRANK. And they can tell just by looking at your teeth?

BETTY. I didn't go to the dentist. I went to Doctor Smedley.

FRANK. And he said...

BETTY. Don't try and talk anymore, Frank, it'll bring your trouble on. I'll see how Father O'Hara's getting on with the tea.

*(She heads towards the kitchen, dejected. **FRANK** stops her.)*

FRANK. Betty?

BETTY. Frank?

(She stops. Beat.)

FRANK. It's marvellous isn't it?

(They hug.)

Look, you better go and have a lie down. I'll bring you up a nice carrot.

BETTY. I'm quite all right. Really! And the BBC are due any minute don't forget.

FRANK. I'm gonna be a father. I'm gonna be a father. I'm a man.

> *(The doorbell rings. In heading towards the door, FRANK trips over his magic case. He gets up and smacks the wall by the door. The doorbell stops but the lamp flickers. He smacks upstage of the door and the lamp explodes, followed by the next lamp, and the next lamp.)*

> *(The timer rings.)*

Dinner's ready!

> *(The oven explodes in the kitchen and various cupboard doors blow open. Mr Rogers bangs on the wall, Jesus drops to the floor, the doorbell rings again and the record player starts with a song in the style of* ["MAGIC"] *by Pilot.*)*

> *(Curtain.)*

---

* A licence to produce SOME MOTHERS DO 'AVE 'EM does not include a performance licence for "MAGIC". The publisher and author suggest that the licensee contact PRS to ascertain the music publisher and contact such music publisher to license or acquire permission for performance of the song. If a licence or permission is unattainable for "MAGIC", the licensee may not use the song in SOME MOTHERS DO 'AVE 'EM but should create an original composition in a similar style or use a similar song in the public domain. For further information, please see Music Use Note on page iii.

ACT II

(Immediately after Act I. **BETTY** *and* **FRANK** *rush into the living room with a waft of smoke. The record is still playing and the doorbell ringing.)*

WELCOME, MR LUSCOMBE

(Between them they turn off the record player, turn the main light on, and re-hang Jesus.)

*(***FRANK*** goes to open the door.)*

FRANK. No wait a minute. *You* should open it so I don't seem too keen,

> *(Switching places.)*

Yes you go first and I'll stand here.

> *(He leans on a banister leg, as if he's propping up the bar.)*

BETTY. Ready?

FRANK. Ready.

> *(***BETTY*** smacks the wall to stop the doorbell. The banister leg comes loose and* **FRANK** *falls through it, just as* **BETTY** *opens the door.)*

BETTY. Mr Luscombe.

MR LUSCOMBE. *(Out of sight.)* Good evening. Mrs Spencer, is it?

BETTY. Do come in.

MR LUSCOMBE. Thank you.

> *(Entering, followed by* **LESLIE** *with the equipment.)*

And this must be *Mr* Spencer.

FRANK. *(Freeing himself, banister in hand.)* Good evening Father Banister – *Mr* Banister – Have you come *far*ther O'Hara Roger Bannister?

MR LUSCOMBE. *(Laughing off this extraordinary behaviour.)* Oh very good. He's started the act and we haven't even said hello yet. Terry Luscombe, BBC Entertainment, pleasure to be here.

FRANK. *(Shaking hands.)* Frank Spencer, Home Entertainment, pleasure to be here too. *(Signaling with the banister by mistake.)* And this is my wife, Betty Bannister – *Spenn*ister – *Benster* Spencer.

MR LUSCOMBE. Pleasure to meet you Mrs Spencer.

BETTY. *(Shaking hands.)* Likewise.

FRANK. *(Shaking hands again.)* Likewise.

BETTY. We've had an eventful day, haven't we Frank?

FRANK. Yes! Betty's going to be giving birth.

MR LUSCOMBE. Oh really?

FRANK. Tonight!

MR LUSCOMBE. Tonight?!

BETTY. Frank *found out* tonight.

MR LUSCOMBE. Gosh!

FRANK. The bank manager told me.

MR LUSCOMBE. Well Congratulations! That's splendid news. Oh, and this is Leslie Robin.

LESLIE. Congratulations.

BETTY. Thank you.

MR LUSCOMBE. Leslie's the man that makes it all work. I just stand there and try to look good.

> *(FRANK laughs. FATHER O'HARA enters from the kitchen with a sooty face. He coughs through a clenched fist and smoke (talc) comes out.)*

FATHER O'HARA. I'm Father O'Hara – nice to meet you.

MR LUSCOMBE. Good evening, Father.

> *(The doorbell rings.)*

BETTY. Excuse me one moment.

FRANK. It's like the hokey cokey in here.

> *(BETTY smacks the door and opens it.)*

BETTY. Oh hello Mum.

MRS FISHER. *(Entering.)* He's gone! He's gone!

BETTY. What do you mean he's gone?

MRS FISHER. David. He's left me.

BETTY. Come on mum, it'll all sort itself out in the morning.

MRS FISHER. It's over. I know it is.

FRANK. *(To MR LUSCOMBE.)* She's in trouble with the bank manager.

FATHER O'HARA. Perhaps Mr Worthington just felt too embarrassed to come back in. Did he say anything to you?

MRS FISHER. He said he was sorry.

FATHER O'HARA. *(Positive.)* There you go!

MRS FISHER. – Sorry he'd wasted his evening.

FATHER O'HARA. Oh dear now.

MRS FISHER. He said it was nobody's fault.

FATHER O'HARA. *(Positive.)* There you go!

MRS FISHER. – but my own.

FATHER O'HARA. Oh dear now.

BETTY. There are plenty more fish in the sea, Mum.

MRS FISHER. I think there's a hole in my net.

FRANK. Mrs Fisher, I'm sorry if I upset things between you and Mr Worthington. Sometimes I can *seem* like a nuisance...

MRS FISHER. I know.

FRANK. But I am the father of your grandchild...

MRS FISHER. I know.

FRANK. And the thing is, I'll always be here.

MRS FISHER. I know.

BETTY. Mum, this is Mr Luscombe and Leslie Robin from the BBC.

MRS FISHER. *(Putting on a brave face.)* Oh. Good evening, gentlemen.

MR LUSCOMBE. *(To* **MRS FISHER.***)* And you must be Mrs Spencer's sister?

MRS FISHER. *(Things are looking up.)* Mmm?

FRANK. No this is Mrs Fisher. She doesn't live here, she just came round for her dinner.

MRS FISHER. I'm Betty's mother. Betty's *single* mother – Betty's *only* mother – Betty's only sole single mother – I don't believe I've had the pleasure of you yet.

MR LUSCOMBE. Lovely to meet you. Terry Luscombe.

MRS FISHER. Would you like a glass of something, Mr Luscombe?

> *(She takes a sip of the prune wine and takes it into the kitchen.)*

BETTY. Yes put the kettle on won't you Mum? I'm sure the gentlemen would like a cuppa.

MR LUSCOMBE. Perfect. Thank you.

LESLIE. Milk two sugars, please, love.

> **(MRS FISHER** *goes into the kitchen.* **LESLIE,** *with the help of the others begins setting up the shot. The banister is replaced.)*

MR LUSCOMBE. Now if you don't mind us grabbing the bull by the horns, let's get going. We've about half an hour, which should be plenty of time, there's nothing complicated, but Leslie and I have another two interviews to fit in this evening so we ought to get a wriggle on.

GOOD LUCK, STUDIO

FRANK. Good luck, studio! Standing by, standing by!

> **(FRANK** *is fidgeting awkwardly.)*

MR LUSCOMBE. Now then: this is quite a CV, Mr... *(Noticing* **FRANK.)** Cramp is it?

FRANK. No *Spencer.*

MR LUSCOMBE. No have you *got* cramp?

FRANK. Oh no I'm just excited.

MR LUSCOMBE. *(Back to the resumé.)* Ah. So, Mr Spencer...

FRANK. F.W.

MR LUSCOMBE. What?

FRANK. My initials. F.W.

MR LUSCOMBE. Oh! Ah.

FRANK. No F.W.

MR LUSCOMBE. I see.

FRANK. No F.W.

MR LUSCOMBE. Oooooooooookaaaaaaaay.

FRANK. Effffffffff Double-Uuuuuuuuu!

MR LUSCOMBE. *(Calmer.)* You are –

FRANK. No –

MR LUSCOMBE. – a magician, a singer, a comic *and* a DIY expert on the side. Not afraid of a challenge then?

FRANK. "Fortune favours the grave".

MR LUSCOMBE. Quite.

> (**LESLIE** *crosses with the sound equipment and tries to get past* **FRANK** *– they end up almost Do-Si-Do-ing.*)

FRANK. He's got a funny walk hasn't he?

MR LUSCOMBE. He's actually got quite a lot of heavy equipment.

FRANK. Oohh.

MR LUSCOMBE. Now if you'd like to sit down with me *here*, and Mrs Spencer if you could join us next to me *here*.

FRANK. *(Concerned.)* No I think she'd better sit nearer the door just in case.

MR LUSCOMBE. In case of what?

FRANK. In case we have to leave in a hurry.

BETTY. I'm not due for another seven and a half months.

FRANK. You can never be sure about these things.

FATHER O'HARA. There's no need to be anxious, Mr Spencer.

FRANK. I can't help it, Father, I'm very worried about my hereditary tendencies.

BETTY. What hereditary tendencies?

FRANK. The Spencers haven't arrived on time for five generations – I come from a long line of early babies. My grandfather was six weeks early, my mother was three weeks early, and I was born very immature.

MR LUSCOMBE. Did you make it to the hospital?

FRANK. Not until tea-time. My mother had me in the afternoon while she was at the pictures watching a John Wayne film.

MR LUSCOMBE. Goodness me. What happened?

FRANK. I think he got shot in the end.

(**MRS FISHER** *enters from the kitchen.*)

MRS FISHER. Sugar, Mr Luscombe?

MR LUSCOMBE. Not for me, thank you, just milk.

MRS FISHER. I was once asked to audition as a dancer for one of your television shows, Mr Luscombe.

MR LUSCOMBE. Oh really?

MRS FISHER. Oh yes. But all my dreams went to pot when I lost my husband.

MR LUSCOMBE. Oh dear, how awful for you.

MRS FISHER. Yes I lost him in the Dartford Woolworths. I was looking for a little angel to go on top of the Christmas tree, and all I found was *him* on top of a *shop assistant.*

MR LUSCOMBE. *(Concerned.)* Dear me. What did you do?

MRS FISHER. I went to British Home Stores.

(She exits to the kitchen.)

MR LUSCOMBE. Now then. Let's sit down shall we? Time flies like an arrow.

FRANK. Mmm. And fruit flies like a banana.

> *(They sit on the lopsided sofa and slowly slide down it.)*

MR LUSCOMBE. Leslie will get your mics on and we'll have an initial chat on the sofa. After that we'll see a bit of your act, and film some shots of you and *Mrs* Spencer as if you're just enjoying a quiet evening at home.

> *(**LESLIE** attaches a microphone to **FRANK**'s lapel.)*

FRANK. *(To **LESLIE**.)* What are you doing to me?!

LESLIE. *(Calmly, moving over to **BETTY**.)* Just giving you a microphone.

FRANK. Don't put your face close to mine!

MR LUSCOMBE. Don't worry, Mr Spencer, just relax.

> *(**LESLIE** is now attaching **BETTY**'s mic.)*

FRANK. And *I'll* touch my wife's personals thank you!

> *(**LESLIE** goes back to the sound case and puts some headphones on.)*

MR LUSCOMBE. Mr Spencer don't worry about it, just relax – relax and *ignore* the camera. In fact I tell you what, if it's all right with you, Mrs Spencer, we'll mention your exciting news at the beginning, just to get us off to a nice start – how's that?

BETTY. All right, yes lovely.

> *(**FRANK** tests his microphone.)*

FRANK. *(Into his mic.)* Hello?

LESLIE. Agh!

MR LUSCOMBE. Please don't do that Mr Spencer.

FRANK. Sorry.

LESLIE. That's one way of knowing it's working.

MR LUSCOMBE. He wasn't to know Leslie. All right it's just a head and shoulders shot so try not to think about it as anything but a casual chat, all right?

> (**LESLIE** *holds a clapper board in front of* **FRANK***'s face.*)

LESLIE. Frank Spencer: Stars of Tomorrow: take one.

> *(Clap.* **FRANK** *shoots up, holding his nose.)*

FRANK. Ow!

> (**MR LUSCOMBE** *pulls him back down.*)

MR LUSCOMBE. All right Mr Spencer.

FRANK. He nearly had my nose off!

MR LUSCOMBE. Calm down, Mr Spencer, it's all right, we'll just keep rolling. *(Back into performance mode.)* Now I'm joined here today by one of our most exciting candidates, Frank Spencer...

FRANK. Good evening.

MR LUSCOMBE. And his wife, Betty.

BETTY. Hello.

MR LUSCOMBE. Frank is of course taking part this series but in fact he and Betty have received some even more terrific news only today, which I'm hoping they might share with me – Frank?

> (**FRANK** *turns to the camera.*)

FRANK. That's right. Earlier this evening we successfully retrieved the news…

LESLIE. Hold it.

MR LUSCOMBE. Sorry hold it there Frank, you're looking directly at the camera, just look at me as if we're having a conversation.

FRANK. Oh sorry.

MR LUSCOMBE. It's all right.

FRANK. I'm a little nervous that's all.

MR LUSCOMBE. Of course. Is it your first time?

FRANK. No I've been nervous before.

MR LUSCOMBE. No is it your first time *on screen*?

FRANK. Oh, yes, yes.

MR LUSCOMBE. Then I understand how you feel.

FRANK. Oh is it your first time too?

LESLIE. We're still rolling, Terry. You can cut straight back in.

MR LUSCOMBE. Now Frank is of course delighted to be a candidate for this series of *Stars of Tomorrow*.

FRANK. Good evening.

MR LUSCOMBE. Good evening – but that's not the only excitement in your life right now, is it Frank?

FRANK. That's right.

(**FRANK** *turns to the camera again.*)

My wife told me this evening, much to my disguise –

LESLIE. Hold it.

MR LUSCOMBE. Stop there, stop there Mr Spencer, you're looking at the camera again.

FRANK. Am I?

MR LUSCOMBE. It's very simple, you just have to keep your eyes on me, okay?

FRANK. But I –

MR LUSCOMBE. Don't over-think it.

FRANK. It's just, when I look into your eyes I get a funny feeling.

MR LUSCOMBE. Well look at Mrs Spencer then, or just to the side of me even. Just don't look at the camera.

FRANK. Just don't look at the camera.

MR LUSCOMBE. Right. Still rolling, Leslie?

LESLIE. Still rolling.

MR LUSCOMBE. All right... Now then, we've a bit of a first here on *Stars of Tomorrow*,

FRANK. Good evening.

MR LUSCOMBE. Good evening... because today, our new candidate Frank Spencer, here now with his wife Betty, has received some very special news. Frank:

FRANK. *(To* **MR LUSCOMBE.***)* Good evening.

> *(Beat.)*

MR LUSCOMBE. Frank, what was it you just told me?

FRANK. Well, this evening...

> *(As* **FRANK** *instinctively turns to the camera,* **MR LUSCOMBE** *grabs his leg, which is out of shot.)*

Oooh...

BETTY. Go on Frank I don't mind.

FRANK. ... My wife told me the knees – the news, that I will very soon...be a candidate for *Stars of Tomorrow*.

MR LUSCOMBE. No. No. No. Cut!

(**FRANK** *looks to the camera.*)

FRANK. For *Stars of Tomorrow*.

MR LUSCOMBE. Not *that*!

FRANK. I didn't look at it once before.

MR LUSCOMBE. Not that *news*!

BETTY. The news of the baby, Frank.

FRANK. He was touching my knee caps.

MR LUSCOMBE. You were looking at the camera.

FRANK. I'm a married man.

MR LUSCOMBE. I am trying to conduct an interview here. On second thoughts, Leslie, I think we'll scrub the interview and let his work speak for itself.

FRANK. But don't you want me to –

MR LUSCOMBE. I don't think we need to worry too much about the interview, it's the act that counts.

(**FRANK** *rushes to change in the cupboard.* **MRS FISHER** *enters from the kitchen with the tea.*)

Let's switch angles, Leslie.

FRANK. Betty could you get my coat?

(**BETTY** *hands* **FRANK** *his coat in the cupboard.* **LESLIE** *moves the camera.*)   *

MRS FISHER. Tea, gentlemen.

MR LUSCOMBE. That's very kind, thank you.

LESLIE. Thanks very much.

MRS FISHER. I was once asked to audition, Mr Luscombe as a magician's ashistant.

MR LUSCOMBE. Oh really?

MRS FISHER. But the night before I saw my husband with another woman at the local pantomime.

MR LUSCOMBE. Oh dear. What an awful thing to experience.

MRS FISHER. Dreadful, but the kiddies love 'em don't they?

(*Beat.*)

FATHER O'HARA. Please excuse me, I think I might take this as my cue to go and get ready. (*To* **MR LUSCOMBE**.) Much as this is most fascinating, I have another engagement this evening at the Civic Hall.

MR LUSCOMBE. Oh, is there a concert?

FATHER O'HARA. No it's a gang show. I thought we should raise some money after the Civic was broken into last month.

MR LUSCOMBE. Right – yes – terrible.

(**FATHER O'HARA** *leans in.*)

FATHER O'HARA. (*Top secret.*) Six and a half thou –

BETTY. Shall I show you the bathroom, Father?

FATHER O'HARA. Don't worry I'll find it myself.

BETTY. It's the first door on the left at the top of the stairs.

FATHER O'HARA. Thank you.

(**FATHER O'HARA** *goes upstairs.* **FRANK** *enters in trench coat and beret from the cupboard.*)

IT'S THE ACT THAT COUNTS

LESLIE. 'Ere. I like your costume.

FRANK. Pardon?

LESLIE. The funny beret and the silly raincoat.

FRANK. I wear this all the time. It was passed down to me. "Silly raincoat".

MR LUSCOMBE. Now then, time for the main event. This is what I've been waiting for.

FRANK. Mr Luscombe, I shall now make your watch disappear in front of your very eye –

MR LUSCOMBE. My watch? Goodness me!

FRANK. – In a trick which I call "Watch Where Your Wristwatch Went".

MR LUSCOMBE. Let's keep rolling throughout this one Leslie, we can piece it together afterwards.

LESLIE. No problem.

BETTY. *(Worried in case the watch gets lost.)* Frank?

FRANK. Yes?

BETTY. Shouldn't you do a different trick? After what happened this morning?

MR LUSCOMBE. "After what happened this morning?"

LESLIE. *(With clapper board.)* Frank Spencer – *Stars of Tomorrow* – take two.

　　　　(Clap.)

FRANK. Ladies and Gentlemen. Welcome – to the world – of Magic Frank:

　　　　(He stamps, and the record player plays. He takes a velvet draw string bag from his pocket.)

Hey diddle diddle! Hey diddle dee!

Examine this magical bag for me.

Alakazam! Alakazee!

Do you not think, it's ord-i-na-ry.

Restaurant*é*. Restaurant*eur*.

Place your watch in the bag, good sir.

O kazongas! O kazingers!

Check it's still there, but mind your fingers.

> *(He snaps the bag shut.)*

MR LUSCOMBE. Agh!

> (**FRANK** *waves the bag around as he casts the magic spell, before opening it for* **MR LUSCOMBE** *to put his hand in.)*

FRANK. Abracadabra! Abracadight!

There's *vanishing* dust in the air tonight.

Abracadabra! Abraca*DOE*!

Is your watch in the bag?_____

MR LUSCOMBE. Yes.

FRANK. Yes?

MR LUSCOMBE. Yes, in fact there are *two* watches.

FRANK. *Two* watches?

BETTY & LESLIE. *Two* watches?

> *(They look to* **FRANK.***)*

FRANK. Tada!

MR LUSCOMBE. Oh cut-cut-cut.

(He stops the record player. **MRS FISHER** *enters from the kitchen.)*

LESLIE. That's a novel disappearing trick.

MR LUSCOMBE. I thought the trick was called "Watch Where The Wristwatch Went".

FRANK. It was.

MR LUSCOMBE. But my watch is still here.

FRANK. That's right.

MR LUSCOMBE. *(Re: Mr Lockwood's watch.)* And who's watch is this watch?

FRANK. This watch...

MR LUSCOMBE. It's extraordinary.

FRANK. This watch...

MR LUSCOMBE. It's covered in diamonds.

FRANK. This watch...

MR LUSCOMBE. Must be worth a fortune.

FRANK. This watch...

MR LUSCOMBE. Well? Where is this watch from?

MRS FISHER. This watch is a swiss wristwatch which Irish witches wear. But if Irish witches wear Swiss wristwatches what watches do Swiss witches wear? So for Irish watches to rest on the wrists of the Irish witches once more, the Irish witches should switch their watches for the watches the Swiss witches wore. Cheers.

(She drinks straight from the bottle.)

FRANK. If you'll excuse me Mr Luscombe, my wife and I need to check something in the kitchen. We won't be a minute.

(They head to the kitchen.)

MR LUSCOMBE. I see – right. Leslie, let's do the arrival shot – we need to get going.

LESLIE. Right.

MRS FISHER. One for the road, Mr Lushman?

WATCH SECRETS

(In the kitchen:)

FRANK. This is Mr Lockwood's watch.

BETTY. I know it is. Why do you need to keep it a secret?

FRANK. Betty, don't you see? If the BBC think I've stolen this watch, I'll be a public embarrassment. We have to get it out of here before the police turn up.

> *(**FATHER O'HARA** enters the kitchen, having come downstairs.)*

FATHER O'HARA. I hope it's all going splendidly. You don't happen to have a spare razor blade by any chance?

BETTY. Yes, Father, there are some in the bathroom cabinet.

FATHER O'HARA. Thank you.

> *(He goes to exit.)*

FRANK. *(Stopping **FATHER O'HARA**.)* Wait a minute, Father.

FATHER O'HARA. Yes?

FRANK. Just before you go. You are not going home now are you not?

FATHER O'HARA. What?

FRANK. You are not, are you not, going home now are you not?

FATHER O'HARA. Not this again.

BETTY. You're going to the Civic Hall now aren't you, Father?

FATHER O'HARA. To the gang show.

BETTY. We wondered if you could give a watch to Mr Lockwood for us?

FATHER O'HARA. A watch?

FRANK. It's rather urgent.

FATHER O'HARA. *(Confused but agreeable. To* **BETTY.***)* Of course. He's expecting it is he?

FRANK. It's a surprise.

FATHER O'HARA. A surprise?

FRANK. On his birthday.

FATHER O'HARA. His birthday?

FRANK. He *wanted* a watch.

FATHER O'HARA. He *wanted* a watch – as a surprise?

FRANK. HAP-py birthday!!!

FATHER O'HARA. Where did you say the razor blades were?

BETTY. In the bathroom cabinet.

FATHER O'HARA. Thank you.

> (**FATHER O'HARA** *leaves the kitchen and goes upstairs.*)

A NORMAL DAY AT HOME

(Back in the living room:)

MRS FISHER. If you want my opinion, Mr Lustman, I've always found it impossible to turn down a gentleman with sideburns and a good polyester suit.

*(**FRANK** and **BETTY** enter. **MR LUSCOMBE** gets up, as **MRS FISHER** falls on the sofa.)*

MR LUSCOMBE. Ah, now then, Mr Spencer, this should be pretty straightforward – I'd like you to wait outside and come, if you will, through the front door, where your wife will be waiting for you.

FRANK. I made that door myself.

MR LUSCOMBE. Oh good. So you'll come into the house...

FRANK. Yes and through my doorway.

MR LUSCOMBE. Yes, yes, and you *ignore* the camera, and you *ignore* me. Just be yourself.

FRANK. Right-oh.

*(**FRANK** goes out the front door.)*

MR LUSCOMBE. And if you wouldn't mind Mrs Spencer, let's have you over here, shall we? And all *you* need to do, if you would, is to wait there to greet your husband as he returns home from work. Just imagine it's a perfectly ordinary, *normal* day in your family life.

MRS FISHER. A normal day. Good luck.

MR LUSCOMBE. Right.

LESLIE. *(With clapper board.)* Frank Spencer: Stars of Tomorrow, Take Three.

(Before he can clap, the doorbell rings – continuously.)

*(**LESLIE** opens the door, **FRANK** comes in, smacks the wall to stop the doorbell and launches into his acting, with **LESLIE** clearly in the shot.)*

FRANK. Hello Betty, I'm home.

MR LUSCOMBE. Mr Spencer.

FRANK. It's me Betty, here I am.

MR LUSCOMBE. Mr Spencer.

FRANK. I walked all the way down the pathway –

MR LUSCOMBE. *(Standing right in front of* **FRANK.***)* Mr Spencer.

FRANK. – and when I got up to my front door –

MR LUSCOMBE. Mr Spencer!!

FRANK. You told me to ignore you.

MR LUSCOMBE. Not when I'm talking to you – Leslie was still in shot. Go back to where you were and wait for me to call you.

FRANK. *(To* **LESLIE.***)* I was all ready to roll, Leslie. Now I'll have to get into the part again.

MR LUSCOMBE. You don't need to get into the part, Mr Spencer. You *are* the part.

FRANK. *(Taking this as a great compliment.)* Oh. Thank you. I'll just go back to where I was shall I?

MR LUSCOMBE. Yes please.

FRANK. *(Revealing his trouser braces.)* Do you think they'll want to see my special braces?

MR LUSCOMBE. No.

> *(Having been off since the end of the first half, the lamp by the door starts flickering.)*

FRANK. That's odd, I thought it was *broken.*

> *(***FRANK*** smacks the wall downstage of the door. The doorbell rings and the light goes off.)*

> *(He smacks the wall higher up – the doorbell continues and light flickers again.)*

(He smacks the wall upstage of the door and the light and the doorbell go off together.)

*(**FRANK** looks at the others.)*

Mmmm.

*(**FRANK** exits through the front door.)*

BETTY. He's had a lot to deal with today.

MR LUSCOMBE. I know the feeling.

MRS FISHER. *(Flirting.)* Are *you* wearing special braces Mr Lumpscombe?

LESLIE. Frank Spencer, *Stars of Tomorrow*, take four.

(Clap.)

MR LUSCOMBE. *(Calling.)* All right then, Mr Spencer.

(Beat.)

(Calling.)

Mr Spencer, we are ready for you.

FRANK. *(Calling from offstage.)* Mr Luscombe, I am ready for you.

MR LUSCOMBE. *(Even louder.)* Come in!!

(Beat.)

*(No sign of **FRANK**. **MR LUSCOMBE** goes towards the door but **FRANK**'s keys start rattling so **MR LUSCOMBE** dashes out of shot as **FRANK** enters.)*

*(Beat, as **FRANK** tries to talk.)*

BETTY. Hello Frank.

*(Beat, as **FRANK** tries to talk.)*

How are you Frank?

(*Beat, as* **FRANK** *tries to talk.*)

MR LUSCOMBE. Hold it!

LESLIE. Cut!

FRANK. Oh, I couldn't find my keys, and then I forgot to ring the doorbell.

MR LUSCOMBE. You don't need to ring the doorbell, you live here!

FRANK. But I couldn't remember my words and I could see you moving in my profiterole vision.

MR LUSCOMBE. (*Raising his voice.*) You don't *have* any words Mr Spencer! It's improvised! All you need to do is to imagine it's been a *perfectly, ordinary, normal, day*, at *work*!!

FRANK. Shouting at me. I'm on the National Health.

MR LUSCOMBE. Now will you please go outside and do it again?

FRANK. Do you think, maybe, you could come with me? Only it would help to know when I am supposed to come in.

BETTY. Mr Luscombe needs to see it from the front, Frank.

FRANK. Oh. Yeah.

MRS FISHER. You know I was *once* asked to audition –

MR LUSCOMBE. Do you know what? I don't think Leslie needs me this side of the camera, so why not?

(*Taking a cigarette.*) It'll give me the chance to grab a breath of fresh air at the same time. Get it rolling Leslie, I'll leave it ten seconds and send him in.

(*They exit through the front door as* **MRS FISHER** *wanders to the kitchen.*)

LESLIE. Frank Spencer, *Stars of Tomorrow*, take five.

> *(Clap. The light flickers again.)*
>
> *(Calling.)*

Hold it!

> *(**LESLIE** follows **FRANK**'s actions and smacks the wall downstage of the door – the doorbell rings and the light goes off.)*
>
> *(He smacks the same wall higher up – the doorbell continues and the light flickers.)*
>
> *(He smacks the wall upstage of the door but as he turns, **FRANK** opens the door and smacks him in the face with it. **FRANK** smacks the wall to stop the bell, closes the door behind him, and carries on, unaware that **LESLIE** is knocked out cold.)*

FRANK. Hello Betty I'm home. Well that was a long day, Betty. I've had meetings coming out of my ears – but guess who's Salesman of the Month!

BETTY. Leslie!

FRANK. No-no-no. Me! Frank!

BETTY. Frank, *Leslie*!

FRANK. Frank *Spencer*. Me – your husband.

BETTY. He's out cold, Frank!

FRANK. It *is* cold out you're right, but we're in a nice warm house with money in the meter and a man on the floor. Oh, is there a leak?

BETTY. He's unconscious!

FRANK. Unconscious?

BETTY. You knocked him out with the door!

FRANK. What was he doing behind the door?!

BETTY. Fixing your lamp!

FRANK. *Now* what's wrong with it?

BETTY. Check he's still breathing.

FRANK. Are you still breathing, Les?

BETTY. No! Check his pulse!

BODY IN THE CUPBOARD

(**MRS FISHER** *tottering in with a glass of wine, sees* **LESLIE** *on the floor.*)

MRS FISHER. A glass of prunes for Mr Louchecombe. Oh, is there a leak?

FRANK. There's no pulse.

BETTY. What?!

MRS FISHER. What?!?!

BETTY. Oh not her as well. Take the glass off her Frank.

FRANK. *(Taking the glass.)* There we are Mrs Fisher.

(**MRS FISHER** *steadies herself on the banister leg.*)

BETTY. He's all right, there *is* a pulse.

MRS FISHER. *(As the banister leg gives way.)* Ohhhh!

FRANK. I'm an innocent man, Betty – but now my career's in jeopardy, your mother's inebriated and Leslie's dead on the carpet.

MRS FISHER. Dead?!

BETTY. He's not dead, Mum, stop panicking.

MRS FISHER. Abbreviated?!

FRANK. I know, you put your mother on our bed to rest, and I'll deal with Leslie.

> (**FRANK** *places the glass on the window sill next to the door.*)

BETTY. All right. Come on Mum, let's get you upstairs. You've had one too many.

> (**BETTY** *starts taking* **MRS FISHER** *upstairs.*)

FRANK. Come on, Les.

> (*He begins to drag* **LESLIE** *into the cupboard.*)

BETTY. What are you doing now?

FRANK. I'm putting him in the cupboard.

BETTY. The cupboard!?

FRANK. Just for the time being. Trust me, Betty.

BETTY. You can't put him in the cupboard.

FRANK. It's only for a minute. If Mr Luscombe hears I knocked him out, my career will be over tonight.

BETTY. What career? Frank, if you carry on like this, you'll be in prison tonight.

FRANK. We'll talk about that in the morning.

> (*The doorbell rings.*)

MRS FISHER. Mr Lovelyman!

BETTY. Mum!

> (**MRS FISHER** *rushes downstairs towards the front door. This is just as* **FRANK** *smacks the wall to stop the bell and opens it, smacking* **MRS FISHER** *in the face.*)

MR LUSCOMBE. (*On doorstep.*) All done?

(Knowing that he has knocked her out,
FRANK *hands* **MR LUSCOMBE** *the glass of
wine from the side.)*

FRANK. There you are, Mr Luscombe. On the house.

(He shuts the door. **MRS FISHER** *is revealed,
out cold.)*

We'll never get her upstairs now. Quickly, let's put her
on the sofa.

BETTY. No Frank I think we should call for an ambulance.

FRANK. We can't do that Betty.

BETTY. Why not?

FRANK. I've broken the telephone.

(The doorbell rings again.)

Look, she'll come round soon, I'm sure. Here, we'll use
this tablecloth to cover her up.

(He tosses the table cloth over her.)

I'll keep Mr Luscombe busy in the kitchen while you
see to Leslie. All right I'll let him in.

*(***FRANK*** *smacks the wall to stop the doorbell
and lets* **MR LUSCOMBE** *in.)*

WHERE'S LESLIE?

MR LUSCOMBE. I presume from the silence that it's all in
the can.

FRANK. Mmm.

MR LUSCOMBE. I thought you'd left me out there for good.

FRANK. Mmm.

MR LUSCOMBE. Where's Leslie?

FRANK. Mmm?

MR LUSCOMBE. Leslie. We ought to be going.

FRANK. That's right, you ought to be going, he must have gone ahead then.

MR LUSCOMBE. What do you mean he's gone ahead? I've been standing outside the front door.

(He points at MRS FISHER.)

What's that?

FRANK. It's a table cloth.

MR LUSCOMBE. *Who* is that?

BETTY. It's my mother, Mr Luscombe.

MR LUSCOMBE. I see. Is she all right?

FRANK. She's having a nap.

MR LUSCOMBE. A nap?

FRANK. Sshh.

MR LUSCOMBE. *(Whispering.)* Under a tablecloth?

FRANK. *(Whispering.)* That's right.

MR LUSCOMBE. *(Whispering.)* Why?

BETTY. *(Whispering.)* Why, Frank?

FRANK. *(Whispering.)* She's having her hair done.

(He whips the tablecloth out to around her neck like a hair salon gown.)

MR LUSCOMBE. *(Whispering.)* Whilst asleep?

FRANK. *(Whispering.)* That's right. Saves time, doesn't it Betty?

(**FRANK** *nods to* **BETTY,** *who reluctantly mimes cutting* **MRS FISHER**'*s hair with imaginary scissors.*)

BETTY. Going anywhere nice on your holidays?

(**MRS FISHER** *mutters sounds of relaxation.*)

FRANK. *(Ushering* **MR LUSCOMBE** *into the kitchen.)* Let's leave them in peace, shall we? You look like you could do with a drink Mr Luscombe.

MR LUSCOMBE. I could *do* with getting going.

(*As* **FATHER O'HARA** *comes downstairs.*)

Father.

FRANK. Father.

BETTY. Come on Mum, let's take you for a rest upstairs.

(**BETTY** *manages to take* **MRS FISHER** *upstairs. In the kitchen:*)

MR LUSCOMBE. *(Following* **FRANK.***)* Where is he then?

FRANK. Who?

MR LUSCOMBE. Leslie!

FRANK. Oh *Leslie*! *That* Leslie. *Leslie*-Leslie.

MR LUSCOMBE. *(Confused.)* Yes?

FRANK. I thought you were referring to the *other* Leslie.

MR LUSCOMBE. What other Leslie is there?

FRANK. You know! Leslie...

(*A fox noise from outside.*)

(*Horrified.*)

The fox!

MR LUSCOMBE. Leslie the fox?

WHAT WATCH?

(The fox is now **FRANK***'s biggest worry.)*

FRANK. *(Looking out the window.)* There he is, the little rascal. Last week I caught him with Mrs Lindbergh and now he could – oh no!

*(***FATHER O'HARA** *enters the kitchen.)*

FATHER O'HARA. Sorry to interrupt but I'm running rather behind time.

MR LUSCOMBE. Have *you* seen Leslie, Father?

FATHER O'HARA. I'm afraid not – could I get that watch off you, Mr Spencer?

MR LUSCOMBE. What watch?

FRANK. What watch?

FATHER O'HARA. The one to give to Mr Lockwood.

MR LUSCOMBE. Mr Lockwood?

FRANK. Mr Lockwood?

FATHER O'HARA. You said it was urgent.

MR LUSCOMBE. Urgent?

FRANK. Urgent?

FATHER O'HARA. For his birthday, you said, he wanted a watch.

FRANK. For his birthday, I said, he wanted a watch... the gang show

FATHER O'HARA. What?

FRANK. He wanted to watch the gang show!

FATHER O'HARA. The gang show? Tonight?

FRANK. For his birthday, yes. He called me – to tell me – to tell you.

FATHER O'HARA. He called you – to tell you – to tell me – well I'll tell him you told me.

FRANK. No don't.

FATHER O'HARA. Don't?

FRANK. You can't.

FATHER O'HARA. Why not?

FRANK. Because...the gang show's cancelled.

FATHER O'HARA. Cancelled? Why?

FRANK. Because of the...

> *(The sound of a fox from outside.)*

> *(Horrified.)*

The fox and the chicken!

FATHER O'HARA. The what?

FRANK. *(Improvising again.)* The Fox and Chicken pub. It caught fire, down the road from the Civic Hall, and all the performers were caught up in it.

FATHER O'HARA. Good grief!

MR LUSCOMBE. Caught up in the fire?!

FRANK. Terrible, isn't it?

FATHER O'HARA. Which performers?!

FRANK. All of them.

FATHER O'HARA. All of them?!!

FRANK. That's what he said.

> *(**BETTY** calls from upstairs.)*

BETTY. *(From upstairs.)* Frank?

FATHER O'HARA. What were the cubs and the brownies doing in the pub?!

FRANK. That's what *I* said!

MR LUSCOMBE. *(Heading through to the living room.)* He told you all this on the phone did he?

FRANK. That's right.

MR LUSCOMBE. On this phone right here?

FRANK. That's right.

MR LUSCOMBE. *(Holding it up.)* This phone that's not even connected!

> *(Beat.)*

FRANK. I'll put it on the list.

MR LUSCOMBE.	**FATHER O'HARA.**
Oh for crying out loud man! What kind of imbeciles do you take us for? I've got other jobs to get to this evening.	What on earth is going on? If the pub's on fire I can't very well start taking watches back to Mr Lockwood.

> *(**BETTY** comes down, exhausted from her exertions.)*

BETTY. Frank? Frank! I'm feeling a bit dizzy.

FRANK. Dizzy? Oh no it's my hereditary tendencies! Don't panic Betty, I'll get you the very best the national health can buy.

BETTY. I'm all right, Frank, it's just a headache, I think.

FATHER O'HARA. *(Heads to the kitchen.)* I'll get you a glass of water, Mrs Spencer.

FRANK. You said it would be seven and a half months, Betty. I'm not prepared. How regular are your contradictions?

BETTY. It's ok Frank, I'm not having contractions.

MR LUSCOMBE. Mr Spencer, there's no need to panic this is quite normal.

FRANK. She could have an undercarriage.

MR LUSCOMBE. Mr Spencer would you calm down! This is a perfectly normal part of any pregnancy.

FATHER O'HARA. *(Turning the tap.)* I think your water's broken.

FRANK. Her waters've broken?!

FATHER O'HARA. No Mr Spencer! The *tap* – the water tap in here is broken.

FRANK. *(Heading to the kitchen.)* Oh no what've you done to it?

FATHER O'HARA. I'm turning it like anyone else would.

BETTY. *(Heading to the kitchen.)* It's all right, Father. Frank – please don't worry! Honestly.

FRANK. *(Realising the problem.)* Oh no!

FATHER O'HARA. What is it?

BETTY. What is it, Frank?

FRANK. I must have turned the water off. Hang on a minute.

(**FRANK** *hammers under the sink.*)

MR LUSCOMBE. *(Bang, bang, bang.)* Mr Spencer. *(Bang, bang, bang.)* Do you really think you *(Bang, bang, bang.)* –

(On the final bang all the lights go out.)

(Beat.)

(Into the kitchen.) Oh surely not!

BETTY. Frank?

FRANK. Okay Father, now twist the tap for me after three?
Ready: one, two, three.

> *(The lights come back up but the pipe has
> burst and* **FATHER O'HARA** *is being soaked
> with water.)*

MR LUSCOMBE. *(Heading in to the mayhem.)* What the
hell are you doing now?

FATHER O'HARA. Turn it off! Turn it off!

FRANK. I can't, I can't, I've burst the pipe.

MR LUSCOMBE. Well turn the water off for God's sake.

FRANK. The cock-stop's above the cupboard, Mr
Luscombe. On the shelf – on the shelf.

MR LUSCOMBE. *(Opening the cupboard.)* What's it doing
up there?

FRANK. But mind the porridge!

> *(As* **MR LUSCOMBE** *opens the cupboard, he
> is late catching the porridge which pours all
> over him.)*

Let me put the cork in.

> *(***FRANK** *puts the wine cork in the end of the
> pipe which has detached itself from the tap.
> Both men are furious.)*

> *(Looking at them.)*

Ooohh.

FATHER O'HARA. I'm supposed to be at the Civic Hall. Look at me!

MR LUSCOMBE. *I'm* supposed to be at another interview. Look at *me*!

FRANK. I'm supposed to be with Mr Lindbergh.

> *(Fox noise.)*

Look at Mr Fox!

> *(On the airer in the kitchen are* **FRANK***'s clothes, which he flings at* **FATHER O'HARA** *and* **MR LUSCOMBE***.)*

Here, gentlemen, there's a change of clothes for you both.

> *(He ushers them upstairs.)*

Chop chop – time is of the essence. Mr Luscombe, I'll go and have a look for Leslie. Father, I'll send a telegram to the Gang Show.

> *(***FRANK*** and* **BETTY** *drag the chicken house from outside back into the living room and places it against the stairs.* **MR LUSCOMBE** *and* **FATHER O'HARA** *ad-lib dissatisfaction as they head upstairs.)*

(From outside, as he comes in.) Shoo! Shoo, rascal, shoo! Come on Mr Lindbergh, I've got you, I've got you. *(To the men, once inside.)* That's right, gentlemen, keep going, keep going – nothing to see here, we've all got places to get to. Father O'Hara turn right and head to the bathroom, Mr Luscombe straight ahead and in to the bedroom.

BETTY. Mother's in the bedroom.

MRS FISHER. *(Screaming in horror from the bedroom.)* Aaahhh!

FRANK. Betty's mother's in the bedroom!

> *(The doorbell rings.)*

Aaahhh! I'll get it, Betty, don't move a muscle.

> *(**FRANK** smacks the wall by the door which stops the doorbell but makes the lamp flicker.)*

> *(He smacks higher up the wall which makes the lamp flicker and the doorbell ring together.)*

> *(He smacks the wall upstage of the door – the lamp goes off, the doorbell stops and the wall light flickers. He walks up the stairs to the wall light and smacks next to it, causing the light to stop flickering and the shelf above him to drop at one end. A box of roller skates falls off the shelf on to **FRANK**'s head. He stumbles forward and gets his leg stuck through the banister.)*

> *(He loses his balance and slides down the stairs crotch-first, knocking out the banister legs like dominoes – stopped only by the final, most painful post.)*

MRS FISHER. *(At the top of the stairs holding the table cloth around her.)* Betty! There's a bedraggled man in the bedroom and he's soaked to the skin. Betty. Betty!

> *(She disappears again.)*

FRANK. I think I've been articulated.

> *(A stunt double for **MRS FISHER** comes out on to the landing, covering her face with her blanket.)*

MRS FISHER. Oh Mr Luscombe it's you! You mustn't see me like this – please – my hair's all over the place.

> (**MRS FISHER** *knocks the top banister over, she falls back into the shelves, and falls straight off the stairs and into the Wendy house. A mass of feathers flies up.*)

> (*Silence.*)

FRANK. Now *that* is not my fault.

> (*There is a knocking at the door.* **FRANK** *opens it.*)

<u>GOOD EVENING, OFFICER</u>

Good evening, officer.

CONSTABLE. Mr Spencer? Thurrock police. I wonder if I might have a word. May I come in?

FRANK. I don't suppose you could come back tomorrow?

CONSTABLE. If you wouldn't mind I'd rather come in now.

> (*He enters.*)

FRANK. Now I know Mr Lockwood sent you, but I only stole it by mistake, Officer, and I'm very sorry.

CONSTABLE. Stole what? Who's Mr Lockwood?

FRANK. You're not here about Mr Lockwood?

CONSTABLE. No, Mr Spencer.

FRANK. Then if Mr *Worthington* sent you, I was unaware of the structural foundations of the house, and I thought the changes were purely anesthetic.

CONSTABLE. I don't know a Mr Worthington either. But I –

FRANK. Mr Luscombe sent you a secret note?

CONSTABLE. Well I –

FRANK. Father O'Hara's issued a complaint?

CONSTABLE. No I –

FRANK. Mr Lindbergh called social services?

CONSTABLE. Mr Spencer, if you'll allow me a word in edgeways, I will tell you why I'm here. Mr Rogers next door is trying to sleep and has been complaining about a couple of strange noises.

FRANK. A *couple*?

CONSTABLE. That's right. I wondered if you'd heard anything.

    (Beat. It happens to be silent.)

FRANK. Nope.

CONSTABLE. No... Funny what the mind can do to you isn't it? Shame, he used to be really on the ball, Mr Rogers. Still, it comes to us all. Don't count your chickens eh?

FRANK. I daren't.

    (The **CONSTABLE** *points at the Wendy House.)*

CONSTABLE. *(Casually, as if off-duty now.)* What's that then?

FRANK. Mmm?

CONSTABLE. *(Jovially.)* That thing. Looks pretty cozy to me. Anyone at home?

FRANK. This, Constable...is the granny flat.

CONSTABLE. The granny flat?

FRANK. Where Betty's mother sleeps when she comes to stay.

CONSTABLE. Really?

FRANK. Yes. That's why I asked you to come back another time. You are in an elderly lady's bedroom.

> (**FRANK** *switches off the wall light.*)

CONSTABLE. *(Embarrassed.)* I see, I see, right, right, well, well, I'll be on my way then. You understand we've got to check all these things out, of course. Anyway, nice to meet you.

> *(A sound comes from the Wendy house: "COCKADOODLEDOO".)*

> *(Turning back.)*

What was that?

FRANK. *(In the same intonation as the rooster, as if it came from* **FRANK.***)* Nice to meet you tooooo!

> *(Another sound comes from the Wendy house: "COCKAYE".)*

Goodbye!

> *(Mr Rogers bangs on the wall.)*

THE RECORD PLAYER

> (**FRANK** *stamps on the floor, and the record player automatically begins with a song in the style of* **["DELILAH"]** *Tom Jones* as the*

---

* A licence to produce SOME MOTHERS DO 'AVE 'EM does not include a performance licence for "DELILAH". The publisher and author suggest that the licensee contact PRS to ascertain the music publisher and contact such music publisher to license or acquire permission for performance of the song. If a licence or permission is unattainable for "DELILAH", the licensee may not use the song in SOME MOTHERS DO 'AVE 'EM but should create an original composition in a similar style or use a similar song in the public domain. For further information, please see Music Use Note on page iii.

door of the Wendy house opens ominously with the music.)

(MRS FISHER *crawls out of the chicken house. She is covered in feathers and, with her autumnal blanket, looks remarkably like a rooster herself. She takes one look at the policeman in uniform and begins dancing seductively towards him.)*

(MRS FISHER *stamps her feet like a matador and the music jumps to a song in the style of* **["KNOCK THREE TIMES"]** *by Tony Orlando and Dawn*. Mr Rogers bangs on the wall and knocks Jesus off it.)*

(FRANK *rushes to put Jesus back, only to meet* **MR LUSCOMBE** *and* **FATHER O'HARA** *on the stairs, dressed identically to* **FRANK**.*)*

(They move down the stairs – by chance in unison – it has the air of a 70s boy band – while **MRS FISHER** *stumbles away into the kitchen.)*

(The three men come down to the living room to greet the policeman – neither quite understanding why they are doing this.)

(Meanwhile **MRS FISHER** *is trying to get a glass of water but can't get the tap to work.*

---

* A licence to produce SOME MOTHERS DO 'AVE 'EM does not include a performance licence for "KNOCK THREE TIMES". The publisher and author suggest that the licensee contact PRS to ascertain the music publisher and contact such music publisher to license or acquire permission for performance of the song. If a licence or permission is unattainable for "KNOCK THREE TIMES", the licensee may not use the song in SOME MOTHERS DO 'AVE 'EM but should create an original composition in a similar style or use a similar song in the public domain. For further information, please see Music Use Note on page iii.

On the appropraite lyric **MRS FISHER,** *by chance, taps on the pipe, which bursts.)*

(Everyone rushes to the kitchen. **FRANK** *leads but the floor is so slippy that he ends up unable to stand up.* **MRS FISHER** *manages to get out of the way.)*

*(***FRANK** *pulls the pulley-airer but it comes off completely and the struts fall out. He puts his head through the hatch to apologise to the policeman but the hatch gives way. There is a building rumble as* **FRANK** *looks up and realises what's coming.)*

(As rubble and dust begin to fill the room, everyone else rushes out. This causes all the lights to overload and go to a blackout, as a final, loud bang sounds.)

(In the darkness the record player strikes back up with a song in the style of **["WITHOUT YOU"]** *by Harry Nilsson*. The lights gradually return to normal revealing a bomb site.)*

*(***FRANK** *emerges from the rubble, becoming aware of* **BETTY** *who is silent and desolate,***FRANK** *starts to live the song, walking across the rubble to his love.)*

---

* A licence to produce SOME MOTHERS DO 'AVE 'EM does not include a performance licence for "WITHOUT YOU". The publisher and author suggest that the licensee contact PRS to ascertain the music publisher and contact such music publisher to license or acquire permission for performance of the song. If a licence or permission is unattainable for "WITHOUT YOU", the licensee may not use the song in SOME MOTHERS DO 'AVE 'EM but should create an original composition in a similar style or use a similar song in the public domain. For further information, please see Music Use Note on page iii.

(*The* **CONSTABLE** *stops the record player and* **MR LUSCOMBE** *turns on the light.*)

WHAT IS GOING ON?

CONSTABLE. I think we'd better all sit down.

(*They all sit.* **FRANK** *is last to sit.*)

(*To* **FRANK.**)

Not you. Would you kindly tell me what is going on?

(*He switches the lights on.*)

FRANK. Where would you like me to start?

CONSTABLE. (*Holding up his dictaphone.*) Where do you think?

FRANK. Well… At the Civic Hall this morning, when meeting Mr Lockwood, I mistakenly misplaced his watch.

CONSTABLE. Right.

FRANK. But I didn't discover the disappearing watch, until the watch I wanted to disappear *didn't* disappear, and the one that *had* disappeared *appeared*.

CONSTABLE. Oh.

FRANK. Now as bad luck would have it, I hit Leslie and Mrs Fisher in the face with the front door, so I put knocked-out Leslie in the cupboard, knocked-out Mrs Fisher in the bedroom, with _locked_-out Mr Luscombe, still left on the lawn outside.

But Mr Luscombe burst in looking for Leslie, Father O'Hara burst in looking for the watch, and the pipes burst on all of us looking for Mr Fox.

Before you arrived, Mrs Fisher jumped into bed with Mr Lindbergh. Then twice on the pipe was too much for the pipe to take, which was too much for the wall to take, and all this is too much for me to take:

Is there a fox in the garden, a chicken in the house or a cow in the oven? First watch, second watch, Irish watch or Swiss watch? Luscombe, Lockwood, Leslie or Lindbergh? I don't know! But if *this* is what you're looking for, you can have it, and there lies the case for the defence.

(He sits, having put the watch in the policeman's hand.)

(Silence.)

CONSTABLE. Oh I didn't press record.

(A calmer, more gathered FRANK.)

FRANK. Constable, I realise that to be holding on to a watch like that is a very bad thing, very bad. But at Christmas this year, my wife will be giving birth, to a baby. And I know I wear my heart up my sleeve, but it really would mean the world to be there. If I don't get a place on your series, Mr Luscombe, I'll understand. If you take away my house, Constable, well it wasn't mine in the first place; But if you take me away from my family –

CONSTABLE. Mr Spencer, I think you misunderstand me. You wouldn't find this watch in the local jewellers. This watch is worth close to six and a half thousand pounds.

FATHER O'HARA. *(The figure sounds familiar.)* Six and a half thousand pounds?

CONSTABLE. That's right, this is the biggest case of embezzlement my department has ever dealt with.

FRANK. Embezzlement?! Embezzlement?! Betty!! What's embezzlement?

CONSTABLE. Mr Spencer, when you performed your disappearing watch routine this morning, you were handling the Civic Hall's stolen funds. Mr Lockwood, the manager, had in fact stolen the money *himself*, and used it to buy this diamond-encrusted watch, which he was planning to flee the country with. Had it not been for your mishap, we'd never've caught him.

FRANK. Mishap? Caught him?

CONSTABLE. That's right. When you left with the watch and Mr Lockwood hit the roof, the stage manager smelt a rat and called me straight away. But, with the evidence gone, you, Mr Spencer, became a second suspect or possible accomplice.

(All gasp.)

Now, Mr Worthington at the bank had alerted us to the missing funds in the first place, and knowing his friendship with Mrs Fisher, I sent Worthington along here earlier to implement plan A.

ALL. "Plan A"?

CONSTABLE. To *find* the watch, without disclosing its value. Of course no watch appeared because you hadn't realised you had it, so Worthington made a swift exit to implement "Plan B".

ALL. "Plan B"?!

CONSTABLE. To have you perform the watch routine once more. If we could arrange a visit from the BBC, it'd be only a matter of time before the watch would show its diamond face, hence the arrival of Terry Luscombe:

MR LUSCOMBE. Otherwise known as *(He whips his wig off)* David Worthington.

(Everyone gasps.)

CONSTABLE. And Constable Robin Leslie. Formerly known as…

> *(Glasses and tache on.)*

… Leslie Robin.

> *(Everyone gasps even louder.)*

FRANK. Mr Worthington. And Leslie! No! Not *the* Leslie! Well I never, Leslie: all this time you've been playing fancy dress, and I thought you were in the closet.

BETTY. But how did you get out without us seeing you?

CONSTABLE. *(Preparing and "talking" into his walkie talkie.)* I made radio contact with my lads around the corner, who in turn forced a brief "power cut" …

> *(All the lights go off. The* **CONSTABLE** *slips behind the chicken house and exits through the secret door.)*

At exactly the time you were fixing the tap in the kitchen.

> *(All the lights come back on. The* **CONSTABLE** *has disappeared. We see the tail end of the front door shutting. Everyone looks to the door.)*

BETTY. Goodness me, and by the time the lights came back on…

FRANK. *(As* **MR WORTHINGTON** *opens the front door.)* He'd escaped.

> *(The* **CONSTABLE** *enters at the top of the stairs.)*

CONSTABLE. That's right.

> *(They all marvel.)*

FATHER O'HARA. *(Getting up.)* They won't believe me at the church when I tell them what I've just witnessed. That was quite something, Constable.

CONSTABLE. I had the men call the Civic Hall to apologise for your absence, Father. I couldn't let anyone leave the premises anyway.

FATHER O'HARA. Oh. Thank you.

CONSTABLE. I'll need you all to file a statement of course, but I'll take those off you individually tomorrow if that's convenient.

FATHER O'HARA. Certainly – anytime, Constable.

MRS FISHER. Oh David, what've you been up to? What've you been up to?

MR WORTHINGTON. Come on, Barbara, I think I better get you home.

MRS FISHER. It was the prunes, David, definitely the prunes.

(They all head to the door.)

FRANK. Before you all leave, everyone, can I just say, I'm sorry about dinner.

MRS FISHER, FATHER O'HARA & MR WORTHINGTON. *(Politely.)* No, no, no, no.

FRANK. Perhaps I could try again tomorrow?

MRS FISHER, FATHER O'HARA & MR WORTHINGTON. *(Rushing out the door.)* No! No! No! No!

> **(MR WORTHINGTON, MRS FISHER** *and* **FATHER O'HARA** *leave hurriedly. The* **CONSTABLE** *is getting his things together.)*

FRANK. Constable Leslie?

CONSTABLE. Yes, Mr Spencer.

FRANK. Not that I'm bothered or anything, and just to confirm of course, but there was no letter from the BBC ...

CONSTABLE. Correct.

FRANK. And I'm not really a candidate for '*Stars of Tomorrow*' ...

CONSTABLE. That's right.

FRANK. And therefore I won't be appearing on the television.

CONSTABLE. Sorry, Mr Spencer.

> (*He goes to leave.* **FRANK** *is at an all time low.*)

However, with Mr Lockwood in custody, the programming's gone to pot at the Civic Hall. There's a short spot in the line-up on Thursday night if you're interested.

FRANK. A spot in the lineup?

CONSTABLE. A short one yes.

FRANK. At the Civic Hall? On Thursday?!

CONSTABLE. I'll get them to call you tomorrow to make the arrangements.

> (**FRANK** *is speechless.* **CONSTABLE LESLIE** *heads to the door.*)

> (*To* **BETTY.**)

I'll be round in the morning to take statements, and I'll bring some of the lads to help clear this place up.

BETTY. Oh Constable – Thank you so much! And I'm very sorry for the inconvenience.

CONSTABLE. All in a day's work. G'night then.

BETTY. Goodnight.

FRANK. Goodnight, Constable.

> *(He leaves.* **FRANK** *and* **BETTY** *come back into the room together.)*

> *(Beat.)*

THAT WENT WELL

That went well.

BETTY. "Well?"

FRANK. In the end I mean.

> *(Beat.)*

I should have left the wall to a professional like you said.

BETTY. Well we'll know for next time eh?

> *(***BETTY*** *sits on the floor, in front of the Wendy house.* **FRANK** *joins her.)*

FRANK. I'm sorry I made such a mess of things. I'm sorry I'm a failure.

BETTY. Frank, you're not a failure. Sometimes you just try a bit too hard – that's all.

FRANK. I only want what's best for you, I promise.

BETTY. I know that, Frank, you *always* want what's best for me. I don't know how I could've have managed it without you.

> *(***FRANK*** *looks at her tummy.)*

FRANK. *(Prudishly.)* Well you couldn't could you?

BETTY. No I mean if they'd taken you away. You've always been here for me, ever since you walked me down the aisle.

FRANK. We had a lovely day for our wedding didn't we? And we're gonna have lots *more* lovely days Betty. Just think, we could be together for another fifty years.

(Beat.)

You know, my mother always said, "Sometimes you find the road of life… Sometimes you…"

*(**FRANK** is upset.)*

BETTY. What is it, Frank?

FRANK. I was just thinking about my mother. If she was here, she'd be a grandmother wouldn't she? That would've been nice.

BETTY. Well, if it's a girl, we'll name it after her.

FRANK. I never really thought about it being a little girl. "Mother Spencer".

BETTY. Her *Christian* name, Frank.

FRANK. Oh, yes. Otherwise they'll think we've given birth to a nun.

(They laugh together.)

"Jessica". That's nice.

BETTY. You're very good to me, Frank.

FRANK. You're very good to me too.

(They kiss. He stands and helps her up.)

Come on, you better get your head down. You go up, I'll be right behind you.

(She heads up the stairs.)

And I don't want you to worry about anything, cause you've got another seven and a half months yet, and if anything goes wrong, you can guarantee I'll be there.

> (**FRANK** *stands alone at the bottom of the stairs, next to the light switch. He surveys the room and picks up a photograph of his mother.*)

"Sometimes you find the road of life has unexpected bends,

But take each corner as it comes, don't worry how it ends.

If things look bad, just go to bed, and dream away your sorrow.

Today may not have been the best, but tomorrow could get worse."

> (**FRANK** *walks up the stairs. He stands at the top and switches off the light. The switch doesn't work so, after several attempts, he bangs the wall and the lights snap out.*)
>
> (*Finale.*)
>
> (*Disco lights fill the room, the front door opens and in come* **MRS FISHER**, **MR WORTHINGTON**, **FATHER O'HARA** *and* **CONSTABLE LESLIE** *all dancing to the music.*)
>
> (*They signal to the top of the stairs where* **FRANK** *and* **BETTY** *appear.* **FRANK** *is dressed in the top hat, white tie and tails that he dreamed of and* **BETTY** *is his glamorous assistant.*)
>
> (*Bows.*)
>
> (*Curtain.*)

ORIGINAL SET DESIGNED BY SIMON HIGLETT

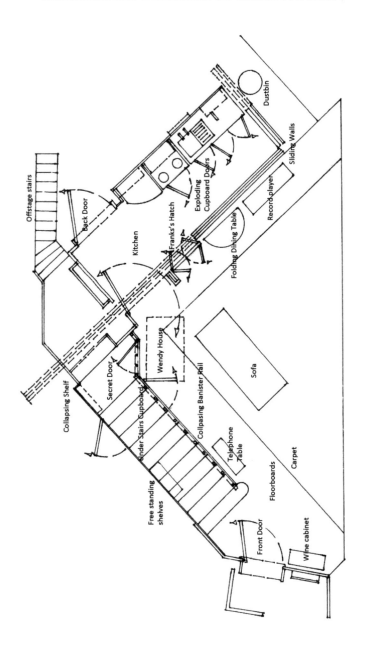

PROPERTY LIST

Plate of pickled apricots
Basic Tea Set for 2
Magic case (strong enough to be sat on)
Telephone bill
Letter in envelope, sealed and addressed to Frank Spencer
Electric kettle
Bottle of homemade Rhubarb wine
Bottle of homemade Prune wine
Tissue box
Tall table lamp on window ledge (with pyro)
Small table lamp on the record player (with pyro)
Standard lamp (with pyro)
Wall light halfway up the stairs
Wooden ironing board
Iron
Table cloth
3x wine glasses
Dictaphone
Box of rollers skates (with soft weight inside)
Framed photo of Frank Spencer's mother
Box of Rice Krispies
TV camera
Tripod
Sound box
3x clip-on microphones wired into the sound box.
Headphones wired into the sound box
Clapper board
Chalk
Cameraman shoulder bag
Red velvet drawstring bag
Diamond ring
Wedding ring
Packet of cigarettes
Chicken feathers
Wall debris
Framed picture of Englebert Humperdinck
Unframed poster of Bruce Forsyth (new print per show)
Smaller framed picture of Jesus.
Homemade Wendy house.
Phone with detachable handset
2x wall shelves (top shelf drops at one end & returns to its starting position)
Flowers in a Chinese vase
Record player with fairy lights around
Tea towel
Tap on sink that squirts
2x corks

2x dinning chairs – one with a leg that breaks
2x fold-out chairs
Sofa – legs drop off one side
Sofa cushions
Wallpaper that rips
Drinks cabinet by the front door (doors fly open and water squirts out)
Dinner table
Egg timer
Shelving unit
Telephone table
Cooker (with pyro)
Coat hooks by the front door
Pulley airer – with brown skirt on it & 2 sets of Frank's shirts and jumpers
Magician's spring cane
Smoke machine for the wall collapse
Bottle of white wine in shop carrier bag
Small leather bag with clothes in for Father O'Hara
Frank's CV
Set of keys
Baking tray with hole in
Staircase (with removable stair spindles)
Rubble drop above kitchen
Practical serving hatch

SOUND EFFECTS

ACT ONE

ACT TWO

LIGHTING EFFECTS

Set practicals

1. Table Lamp on record player
    On top of record player in living room
2. Coloured Fairy lights
    Wrapped around legs of record player
3. Record Player
    Display light in record player
4. Wall lamp
    Just DS of the shelf on the stairwell wall pointing downstairs
5. Standard lamp
    Against US wall between secret door and stair cupboard
6. Table lamp in window
    On windowsill of SR window DS of front door

Effects and locations

1. Smoke machine behind SL kitchen wall
    For oven smoke effects coming either through oven or the USL
    kitchen back door
2. Smoke machine behind secret door
    Only used for wall collapse in Act 2
3. Pyro – Oven
    Set on top of oven
4. Pyro – Table lamp on record player
    Set just behind table lamp on record player
5. Pyro – Standard Lamp
    Set directly on standard lamp
6. Pyro – Table lamp in window
    Set in bottom of lamp base facing the stage

LIGHTING EFFECTS

ACT ONE

ACT TWO

ABOUT THE AUTHOR

Guy Unsworth is primarily a freelance theatre director based in London, working in the UK and internationally. Guy grew up in Southport, Lancashire, and after studying Industrial Economics at the University of Nottingham, won the Directors Guild of Great Britain award for Best New Director at the National Student Drama Festival.

Following postgraduate training at the Mountview Academy of Theatre Arts, he worked under the mentorship of Christopher Luscombe, Hannah Chissick and Lucy Bailey, as Assistant and Associate Director on numerous productions in the West End and at the Royal Shakespeare Company.

Guy's freelance career now spans a wide range of genres, from new musicals to Shakespeare.

As an author, Guy is a co-bookwriter with Alain Boublil (*Les Misérables, Miss Saigon*) for the 2012 revival of *Marguerite*, and devised the narrative for the West End hit Cool Rider. *Some Mothers Do 'Ave 'Em* is Guy's debut play script.

Directing credits include: *Bring It On* (Southbank Centre); *The System* (screen); *My Fair Lady* (Grange Festival Opera & The Liceu, Barcelona); *Being Mr Wickham* (screen); *Julius Caesar* (Fort Canning Park, Singapore); *Of Mice and Men* (UK Tour); *Some Mothers Do 'Ave 'Em* (UK Tour); *Hand To God* (Singapore Repertory Theatre); *Moving Stories* (Haymarket, West End and Houses of Parliament); *The Food of Love* (Cadogan Hall, Royal Festival Hall); *Cool Rider* (Lyric & Duchess, West End); *The Collector, Death and the Maiden* (English Theatre Frankfurt); *Cinderella* (Manchester Opera House, Nottingham Theatre Royal); *Snow White* (Manchester Opera House); *A Night with Bonnie Langford* (London Hippodrome, Richmond Theatre); *Farragut North* (Southwark Playhouse); *Sweet Smell of Success, Company* (Arts Ed); *Marguerite* (Tabard); *Fresher the Musical* (Pleasance, Islington and Edinburgh); *Someone Who'll Watch Over Me* (Cockpit); *Play-in-a-Day Series* (London Bridge Tunnels); *Metamorphosis* (British American Drama Academy); *The Bear Who Paints* (Pleasance Edinburgh); *Proof* (NSDF Finals). Other titles: *Made in Dagenham, Billy, The Ghost Train, Into the Woods, Humble Boy, Disco PIgs, Company, Guys and Dolls, Merrily We Roll Along, Thoroughly Modern Millie, Lucky Stiff,* and *The Laramie Project*.

For more information, go to guyunsworth.com

ABOUT THE ORIGINAL WRITER

Raymond Allen was born on the Isle of Wight, where he still lives, Raymond was a reporter, then joined the RAF and later did various part-time jobs, including dishwashing, while attempting to become a full-time writer.

After twelve years of rejection, and being told by a script reader that he had no sense of humour or talent, he was working as a cinema cleaner when he broke into television by writing comedy material for Frankie Howerd and Dave Allen.

Then Raymond had an idea for a comedy series about a couple called Frank and Betty Spencer. It was offered first to Norman Wisdom, who didn't see any humour in it and having seen a complete script said he supposed Raymond put the funny bits in later! Ronnie Barker also turned it down, as did everyone else. Then a young actor called Michael Crawford, who had previously starred in the Hollywood musical *Hello, Dolly!*, saw the script. He liked it and so, with Michele Dotrice as Betty, *Some Mothers Do 'Ave 'Em* finally came to television. It ran for twenty two episodes and was the BBC comedy entry in the Golden Rose of Montreux Festival in Switzerland. At its peak, it reached an audience of 25 million and has now been shown in over 60 countries. Raymond has also written short stories for radio, a novel, comedy sketches for the BBC and ITV, and his first stage play, *One of Our Howls Is Missing*, starring Christopher Beeny, was presented at the Haymarket Theatre, Leicester, in 1979, followed by a national tour. In 2016, after an absence of 38 years, Frank Spencer returned to television in a 15-minute special for BBC's Sport Relief, which Raymond co-wrote with the Dawson Brothers.

www.ingramcontent.com/pod-product-compliance
Ingram Content Group UK Ltd.
Pitfield, Milton Keynes, MK11 3LW, UK
UKHW020812070325
455964UK00015B/241

9 780573 115509